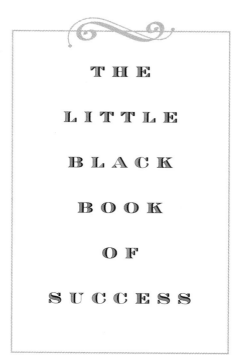

THE
LITTLE
BLACK
BOOK
OF
SUCCESS

· ·

ELAINE MERYL BROWN,

MARSHA HAYGOOD,

AND RHONDA JOY McLEAN

Foreword by Angela Burt-Murray

· ·

ONE WORLD | BALLANTINE BOOKS | NEW YORK

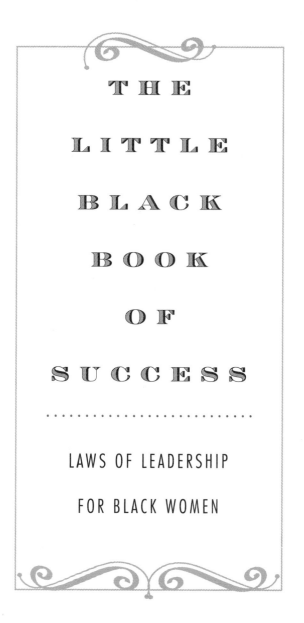

THE LITTLE BLACK BOOK OF SUCCESS

LAWS OF LEADERSHIP

FOR BLACK WOMEN

Published in the United States by One World Books,
an imprint of The Random House Publishing Group,
a division of Random House, Inc., New York.

ONE WORLD is a registered trademark and the One World
colophon is a trademark of Random House, Inc.

ISBN 978-0-345-51848-4

Printed in the United States of America

www.oneworldbooks.net

2 4 6 8 9 7 5 3 1

First Edition

Book design by Jo Anne Metsch

31232009054539

*To black women who continue to climb
the leadership ladder and those who have
been there to support them.
You are all VIPs.*

CONTENTS

*High self-esteem is a cornerstone to success: Overcome
feelings of inferiority despite regularly being
referred to as a minority.*

*Use the tools you know—prayer and affirmation—to control
and change your thoughts. Also, learn new methods
to develop a leader's mental attitude.*

*Even the best managers can succumb to unconscious
stereotypes or implicit prejudice. You must understand
the perceptions of the dominant culture and your
biculturalism if you want to succeed.*

*Resist your tendency to take on the role of caregiver,
a role that may not help you in your pursuit of
being perceived as a leader.*

leader, it's critical to have superb verbal and written
communication skills.

Don't confuse your net worth with your self-worth.
The talents you acquired as a leader in your community,
church, or school have value in the workplace—
apply them!

Not only is self-evaluation important, but what your boss
thinks about your work also impacts your leadership pursuits.

Perception is reality: Put your best foot forward
and make the best impression.

You don't have to be the same race, gender, age, or religion
to build a success team of people you can count on
for guidance and mentorship.

Networking can expand your support system.

Cross over into other cultures for social
and professional growth.

The Ostrich Syndrome and how to avoid it.

FOREWORD

Tapping into Your Leadership Potential

What separates merely good managers from great ones? Anyone will tell you they've probably worked for effective managers as well as a few bad apples. During my own career I've had bosses that micromanage their employees, those who expect everyone else on the team to do all the work while they take all the credit, and those rare jewels that support their employees, help them develop strategic goals, and know that when one person succeeds the entire team succeeds. These great leaders also embrace and encourage hard work for themselves and their teams and don't look for shortcuts to a win. Whether you are just starting out on your career path, stuck in a mid-level rut, or preparing to ascend to the executive corner office, understanding the difference between "just managing" people and leading them effectively will determine how quickly you move to the next level in your career. Given the screaming headlines of corporate mismanagement that are perpetually pervading the marketplace, strong, authentically centered leadership skills are more important than ever.

Your first step in striving for excellence, moving past self-defeating behaviors, and bursting through what may seem like impenetrable barriers is to read *The Little Black Book of Success: Laws of Leadership for Black Women.* Chockful of sage pearls of wisdom from co-authors Elaine Meryl Brown, Marsha Haygood, and Rhonda Joy McLean, this book will provide you with practical steps to enable you to tap into your own leadership potential. These three dynamic, driven, and successful women have collectively honed their leadership skills with a combined total of nearly 100 years of senior management experience at Fortune 100 companies and leading nonprofits and grassroots community organizations. Their book will enable you to discover and develop your own leadership potential and move yourself forward.

The Little Black Book of Success's chapters are each built around a core principle or "law," with historical context, real-world examples, some traps to avoid, and "MAMAisms"—those things we all learned at "Mama's knee" that have gotten us through life and that you can still rely on as you take your rightful place as new leaders. No matter where you are in your own career path—whether you want to strengthen your self-esteem, learn to build an effective network, deal with challenging environments and co-workers, or learn the best way to develop your own leadership style—*The Little Black Book of Success* will give you the real-world tools and tips you need in order to navigate your career pathways successfully.

As Elaine, Marsha, and Rhonda point out, women of color who are executive leaders often face unique challenges, and have to dig deep within themselves to find ways to blossom under the intense pressures of their positions. The strength and decisiveness that helped them evolve into the leaders they have become can be yours as well, and you, too, can embark upon your own unique leadership journey.

When the nation first met First Lady Michelle Obama on the campaign trail she was instantly recognizable to Black women. The statuesque, double Ivy-league degreed hospital executive with the perfectly coiffed hair and smart outfits was a self-made woman like many of you who lead church boards, chair neighborhood programs, and rush home from work to feed their families. Even under the intense scrutiny she faced, by remaining true to the values, lessons, and ideals she developed when growing up in her home on the South Side of Chicago, Mrs. Obama was able to address the criticism of her in the press while remaining focused on her family and her passion for community service and opening up the White House to the American people.

The lesson here, that is underscored in *The Little Black Book of Success*, is that no matter where you are in your career and what obstacles you feel you must overcome, if you are clear about, and remain committed to your core values, those that you learned in your own homes and communities, you can survive and thrive as a leader, even when people attack you and try to throw you off course. Truly effective leadership is a combination of learned experience and innate ability. As Elaine, Marsha, and Rhonda write, "Leadership can be learned." Couple your innate ability with the practical, insightful, and motivating material in *The Little Black Book of Success* and you will have all the tools you need to become the best leader that you can possibly be.

ANGELA BURT-MURRAY
Editor in chief
Essence magazine

INTRODUCTION

Although they're able to get jobs, many of today's young Black women don't realize they have the potential to move themselves forward. It's interesting to note that many Black women hold leadership roles in their communities, schools, and churches, but aren't aware that they can transfer skills from those leadership positions to the workplace. Research indicates that their talents often remain invisible both to the women who possess them and their business managers.

But leaders are not only born, they can be made. Leadership can be taught, and you can learn to unleash your leadership abilities with the help of this book. This is a guide that will give all sisters who aspire to be "players" a way to get into the game and stay in the game. Whether you know it or not, once you're in the workforce you're already in the game, so you might as well play your "A" game.

Each of us has a personal reason for writing this book. Our different roads led us to this intersection. Our different journeys brought us to the same place—that place in our careers where we are ready to share knowledge of our experiences with sisters young and old to help them tap into their leadership potential and navigate through any organization, corporation, or institution.

ELAINE'S STORY

In early 2000, an HBO Human Resources' executive invited me to attend my first leadership class—the Executive Leadership Development Program sponsored by NAMIC—the National Association for Multi-Ethnicity in Communications. It turned out to be a program that changed my life. As a creative director in this class of mostly business/marketing students, it was the first time ever that I saw myself as a leader. With an opportunity to identify my own leadership skills, learn new leadership skills, and tap into my leadership potential, it was there I had my "Aha!" moment: Leaders are not just born; leaders can be made. There are leadership skill sets and rules that can be taught just as grammar is taught in english and fractions can be taught in math. After taking this class and the whole notion of leadership seriously, I set out to put what I learned into practice and reached out to form my own support network and mentors. Getting together a few colleagues across Time Warner divisions, I gathered a group of Black women executives for dinner; among them were Marsha Haygood and Rhonda Joy McLean. We met every quarter at dinners that became known as Girls Night Out, or "GNO" dinners. Still excited about my leadership experience, I wanted to write about it and share my "Aha!" moment with others who might not have tapped into their leadership potential. After several attempts at a treatment for a book on leadership and several rejections, I realized that this book was much bigger than me, that I couldn't write it on my own. Not losing sight of how much value a book like this would have for Black women, I asked the members of GNO if they would like to participate in the writing project. As a result, Marsha and Rhonda, also passionate and committed to sharing their thoughts and experiences, were up for the task. It was the beginning of a great collaboration that would bring ninety collective years of leadership experience to *The Little Black Book of Success: Laws of Leadership for Black Women.*

MARSHA'S STORY

I have been a trailblazer, considered the "first lady" and "only lady" in more situations than I can count as I've journeyed along my career path from temporary, part-time receptionist to executive vice president. In many of the situations that I encountered along the way, I have had to rely on the confidence and self-esteem I built from my mother's encouragement and the support of my family. Often I had to dig deep and rely on my mother's words that I could "do anything I put my mind to."

During my twenty-five-plus years in the corporate arena, I have experienced some difficult situations and injustices, but for the most part, there have been more good situations than bad ones, and I have tried to learn from all of these experiences. For many years during my climb up the corporate ladder, I was one of the "only." Now as a career coach and small-business owner I want to share some of the lessons I learned along the way. We all know that there is no one guidebook to a successful career, but my hope is that this book will offer insight and support to women who do not always have access to coaches, mentors, or the "Old Boys' Network."

RHONDA'S STORY

From the time I was thirteen and integrated the local high school in my small Southern town with two of my best friends, I have benefited from my family's unwavering support and the "home training" that they provided. That grounding and spiritual foundation have served me well, enabling me to obtain four degrees, culminating with my J.D. from Yale Law School in 1983. After working in the not-for-profit sector for nearly ten years before attending law school, I have been a practicing attorney for more than twenty-five years and have experience in the public, private, and academic sectors, working my way up from entry- or midlevel management posts in each of those arenas. I have observed and participated in many changes in our society, including major advancements and additional opportunities for women and people of color. Even so, I still see young women making avoidable mistakes as they climb the corporate ladder. It is my hope that the leadership lessons in our book will help those women find their place at the senior management table and become the next generation of leaders in Corporate America and the world at large.

Those are our stories, and now here's the big picture behind

THE LITTLE BLACK BOOK OF SUCCESS:
LAWS OF LEADERSHIP FOR BLACK WOMEN.

Given how much progress women of African descent have made since the civil rights and women's rights movements—especially in the past decade, as companies have grown more diverse—it would be easy to think challenges in the workplace don't exist. Wrong! Nearly 40 percent of Black women report that they don't have other Black women who can serve as role models. Studies show that during the past decade Black women have made the smallest gains with regard to employment and high-level positions. For the few who have achieved success in the workplace, their greatest obstacle has been making their organizations acknowledge the value of their skills and contributions.

Today's Black women have jobs and careers, yet many don't realize the inherent leadership potential they possess that can help them grow professionally. Much has been written about leadership, but there are no books specifically for Black women on this topic, one that identifies and addresses issues unique to Black women, the workplace obstacles they encounter, and challenges they can overcome.

As women of color, we live in a culture that is part of a larger society—a dominant culture. Each culture has its own set of mores, traditions, and values. These values, attitudes, and ideologies that are inherent in our communities have been passed down through generations and make our culture unique, particularly given our people's historical experiences in this country. This book identifies some things we tend to do that may differ from the dominant culture as we operate in the corporate workplace. Rather than focusing on assimilation, we think it is more important that you understand your own behaviors and how they may work for or against you, so that you can maximize your leadership potential. Let's face it. We're all bicultural—having our own culture within a dominant culture. This handbook provides insights into understanding how you can become more self-aware and achieve your leadership goals.

Beginning with the premise that we're all VIPs with differing degrees of awareness, *The Little Black Book of Success* shares insights into workplace issues, pitfalls, and impediments, and offers applicable solutions for women, no matter at what stage of their career.

Each chapter builds on the VIP lessons by elucidating leadership truths coupled with prescriptive examples. We talk about the behaviors we have observed in the workplace that work to our advantage and those that keep us from advancing. The Cultural Code sections include the kinds of things we tend to do from a cultural perspective to sabotage ourselves and then prescribe methods to help us be successful.

Each chapter concludes with "MAMAisms," which bring the lessons home by giving entirely new relevance to aphorisms readers have heard all of their lives from their mother, grandmother, or other family members, presenting them in the context of leadership development. The premise here is that even if Mama was not in the corporate world, she gave us life lessons we can draw upon. MAMAisms are those familiar terms, both practical and spiritual, that we grew up with and can draw upon as we travel the road to leadership success.

We hope that this isn't a book you read once and store on your bookshelf, leaving it to collect dust, but one that you keep on hand and review regularly to help you reach your leadership goals or serve as a reminder of what to do when things get tough.

We have been working a long time in many different jobs and industries and have tried to learn from our mistakes as well as our achievements as we advanced in our careers. Our combined experience can help you avoid making some of the mistakes we made as you build a strong foundation of professionalism in your work and develop the tools you will need for leadership success.

So, whether you are just starting out in the workplace or already have a leadership role, get ready to change your life!

PERSONAL LEADERSHIP NOTEBOOK

We strongly recommend that before you begin reading *The Little Black Book of Success*, you create a Personal Leadership Notebook (PLN) that you can use to jot down your insights and ideas as you work your way through the book. Your PLN will become your personal journal, your diary, your bible, which you will write in as needed. It is best to get a notebook with a folderlike flap so you can tuck newspaper clippings, magazine articles, network programs, or documents inside that you want to save and reference at a later date. Your PLN will track your progress, and it will be a place where you can keep contact information, important dates, project results, and any other data relevant to your leadership journey. Your PLN should be dog-eared from much use and handling from going in and out of your purse, handbag, and/or briefcase. Each year when you buy a calendar, you should buy a new PLN, which means as you grow along your leadership journey, so should the number of your PLNs. We will refer to the PLN from time to time so remember, you heard it here first! Go now and get this notebook that you will use to chart your way to leadership success. It doesn't matter what it looks like—an old diary that you never wrote in or a brand-new colorful journal—you will want to carry your PLN around with you so that you can use it often and make it work for you. Read this book from front to back while taking notes in your PLN, then read it through a second time, taking more detailed notes, perhaps this time around, starting to develop your action plan.

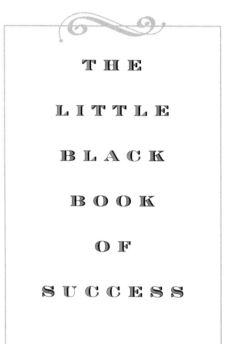

THE

LITTLE

BLACK

BOOK

OF

SUCCESS

Always Consider Yourself a VIP

Many of you are already active in the workplace or will soon be entering workforces all over the world—in privately held corporations, large foundations, small not-for-profit organizations, advocacy groups, government positions, or other jobs right in your neighborhood—and yet, you may not know a very important secret: There is a leader inside each of you just waiting to come out! All you need to do is develop and hone the skills that will help the leader in you to surface and shine.

Leaders are not only born, they can also be created. Even if you have never held a leadership position and were told that you did not have "leadership potential" as you were growing up, you can learn what it takes to be a leader right now. Like math, science, and languages, leadership can be learned because it requires skill sets that can be taught. And since you are clearly capable of learning, the path to leadership is one you can always pursue.

However, along the path to leadership success, you will have to refuse to give in to negative thinking that can hold you back. Too often brilliant and beautiful young women of color sabotage themselves, sometimes without even knowing that they are doing it, so that they never become the leaders they are capable of becoming or achieve the level of leadership success they deserve. **The most critical aspect of leadership is self-esteem, which must flow from the core of your being.**

In order to become a leader and remain an effective one, you must always consider yourself a Very Important Person (VIP). This doesn't mean that you should be arrogant or cocky and walk into your job believing that you already know everything you need to know. Instead, it means that you need to feel confident that you are bringing much value to any workplace and that your cultural strengths, values, and work ethic will stand you in good stead as you go about learning how to do your job, and that you will be successful despite any challenges you may face, whether they are small or large.

How you feel about yourself is imperative to moving forward and sustaining your efforts to meet your leadership goals. Feeling that you're a VIP, reminding yourself that you're a VIP, dressing like you're a VIP, and acting like you're a VIP (within reason, of course) will help to give you the confidence you need to conquer real and imagined obstacles in your workplace. Rest assured that you can overcome any hurdles you may encounter on your way to becoming a leader—just be prepared and hang on to your hat. External—and maybe even internal—forces will surely test you.

Because we live in a society where people of color and women are not always valued, some of us consciously or subconsciously transfer the notion that we are not valuable to beliefs of inferiority or inadequacy about ourselves.* A recent Harvard University study identified two kinds of prejudice: individual and systemic. The first kind of prejudice is held by individuals about members of groups other than their own. The second is a set of institutionalized assumptions, attitudes, and practices that have a kind of invisible effect in systematically giving members of more powerful groups certain advantages over members of less dominant groups. **So you**

*"How Unethical Are You?" Mahzarin R. Banaji, Max H. Bazerman, and Dolly Chugh, *Harvard Business Review,* 12, 2003.

are not crazy, and you are not alone in feeling that some things are not right or fair in our society. Despite all of the progress women and people of color have made, there are still obstacles in many workplaces. Therefore, you must be ready.

The first step to handling any sense of unfairness in the business environment is to accept that prejudices of all kinds exist. Indeed, many of us are prejudiced, and instead of letting these feelings get in your way, you must find creative ways to move around them. You may feel frustrated at times, not knowing how to get ahead or what steps you should take to advance. **You're not alone. Don't be discouraged.** Instead, concentrate on working hard, working smart, and gaining the knowledge you need to move forward. By remaining focused, you will continue to make progress.

Your ability to remain motivated and continue to believe in yourself as you travel along your leadership journey is very important. In the sport of working, you will need to learn not to take personally everything that happens to you. You must become a savvy "player" in the work "game." Once you decide to become a leader, you put yourself squarely in the game and you must play. You must also be prepared to win as well as suffer some losses along the way. Often those wins and losses will yield critical lessons that will help you mold your own unique leadership style that will make you stand out and move up. Be prepared for the rules of the game to change, sometimes midplay, sometimes completely. Make it your responsibility to keep up with what is going on. Plan to put your own special imprint on your workplace by bringing the very best you have to the table every day. Always hold your head high and remember that you are a VIP, no matter what position you currently hold. You're already on your way to leadership success!

CULTURAL CODE

Given our country's history of legalized slavery, indentured servitude, and the treatment of women as chattel and children as possessions, we should not be surprised if occasionally some of us buy in to notions that we are not worthy, that we are undeserving, that we are second best. As a subculture within a dominant culture, we may see more negative than positive reflections of ourselves being portrayed in the media. And in the workplace we may see other employees who don't look like us advance more rapidly than we do (and sometimes they don't have half the credentials and experience that we have) and we may wonder why.

While there are nearly always things we could do differently or better in our jobs, we all know or have heard of situations where other workers we may have welcomed to the company and trained have received promotions instead of us or much sooner than we do, or co-workers who have gone overbudget on their projects while we have stayed within our budgets, yet they have been promoted and we have remained in our positions. We have met "hotshots" who seem destined to shoot to the top of the department or company no matter what they do or how many failures they produce. This process is often referred to as "failing up."

These experiences can be discouraging, but they can also be motivating. We must learn that everything we are going through is all a part of the game—surviving and thriving in the workplace—and the sooner we face this reality the better we will be able to compete in the leadership arena. We must keep our confidence intact and realize that outer forces have nothing to do with our inner spirit—our resilience—that we inherited from our MAMAs and others. We stand on the shoulders of our ancestors, who sacrificed mightily so that we could have the privileges and opportunities we take for granted today. Through them we know and affirm that we are amazing women, and with confidence in ourselves, we can do anything!

 **MAMAisms**

- ○ Nothing worth having comes easy.
- ○ You have to work twice as hard as everyone else to get anywhere.
- ○ You are worthy and deserving of having the best of everything.
- ○ Make yourself number one.
- ○ If you don't take care of you first, no one else will.

To Attain Victory, Stay Positive

Master the art of positive thinking. To become a leader you must have a positive mental attitude, which you can achieve with positive self-talk and looking at what is right with people instead of what is wrong with them. Positive self-talk means saying positive things about yourself to yourself and to others. You are what you think, and you can accomplish what you think you can. For example, if you tell yourself that you can't perform a particular task or difficult assignment, then you are setting yourself up for failure. You must tell yourself that you can meet professional challenges that come your way. Instead of thinking, "Oh, I can't do this. I've never done this before," say, "This is new to me. I'll give it my best shot." Then go do your homework, consult with others, go online, request the reports, do whatever you need to do to get the information to complete the assignment to the best of your ability. Positive thoughts create constructive energy around you.

You must establish this habit of positive self-talk in your mind, because it requires regular reinforcement. **Make it a habit.** Invest five minutes a day before you head out to work. Tell yourself you can meet any professional challenges that life has to offer. Write down your positive affirmations in your Personal Leadership Notebook and read them out loud, or write a positive prayer. The spoken word is extremely powerful.

For example:

- I release the past and now allow myself to be filled with positive thoughts.
- I deserve the best and welcome it into my life.
- I see the good in everyone.
- I accept for myself all the good things that life and work have to offer.
- I am worthy and deserving of new challenges that come my way.
- I am in the process of making positive changes.

Be actively aware of what you're thinking. What kind of voice do you hear in your head? Does a voice tell you that you can't do something because a family member warned years ago that you were going to fail? Or that trying something new was too risky? Or that traveling abroad or to other parts of the country is dangerous? If you begin to see a pattern of negative thoughts, write them down and then create positive affirmations to cancel them. You must reprogram your thoughts. It's the only way good things are going to come to you in life. You can make it a good day or a bad day by controlling your thought process. Even if something bad happens to you during the day, you can decide how to react to the situation. Your reaction is your choice and your choice determines how you will respond—positive or negative. Create positive images, statements, situations, outcomes, interactions, and exchanges. You can change your life if you change your thinking.

Having a sense of humor also comes in handy and can help you with your positive attitude. There will be times when you'll just have to throw up your hands and laugh.

Negative self-talk can lower your expectations, and do damage to your self-confidence and leadership ability. People want to follow leaders who are positive. One of a leader's most important jobs is to set a positive tone.

People who are positive tend to be:

- More productive at work.
- More likely to be noticed and recognized by their boss.
- More likely to attract co-workers to them.
- More likely to be open to new experiences.
- More likely to recognize opportunity when it comes their way.

CULTURAL CODE

We haven't always been exposed to positive images in life, whether due to the media or the racial divide. Not everyone was raised by supportive or well-educated or instructive parents. We haven't always been around positive family and friends. While growing up, some of us didn't receive the attention and encouragement we deserved in classrooms from teachers. While our parents were sometimes struggling to make ends meet, or being challenged by more obstacles than we experience today, we haven't always had the most positive view of the world. Unfortunately, we can even be negative about ourselves. Sometimes we assume that the challenges we are facing have been set before us because we are Black or women. While this may or may not be true, we may become paralyzed with anger or fear because of our own beliefs. We can get in our own way by deciding that "they're out to get me," or "they just don't understand or value me," and that nothing can be done about it. Look beyond skin color and don't focus on it. We cannot let differences, or what others think or feel, get in the way of achieving our leadership goals. Despite the negative forces around us or inside us, we must overcome them as we embark upon this journey. We have to be positive and view the world in a positive light. For not to be positive would be to give up all hope. We are a strong and spiritual people. We have survived through the ages with physical strength and the strength of our minds. Negative thinking that creates negative emotions can lead to stress, anger, and hostility, as well as disease. So keep your thinking positive.

Write a list of your good qualities and assets in your PLN. Place positive messages to yourself around your home, tape them to your dresser and medicine cabinet mirrors. Read them out loud and often. Carry them with you in your purse and keep them in your desk drawer at the office and refer to them as a reminder whenever necessary. Refresh or update these positive messages or affirmations to yourself on an as-needed basis. Even if you've been in your position for years, look at today as if it's your first day on the job and immerse yourself in positive thinking.

 MAMAisms

○ **There's nothing in the world you can't do once you put your mind to it.**
○ **Always take the high road.**
○ **Stay on course and expect to be successful.**
○ **Positive energy yields a positive attitude.**
○ **Hold your head up high.**

Racism Is No Excuse,
but It Can Be a Motivator

As a Black women in America, you will be confronted by or exposed to racism, but instead of getting angry, letting it defeat you, get the best of you, keep you down, prevent you from growing, exploring, realizing your full potential, and manifesting your dreams, use racism as a motivator to accomplish your goals.

Allow the racism that exists to move you in a forward direction and make you all the more determined to achieve your goals so that no outside forces throw you off balance and make you lose focus on what it is you set out to achieve. In this case, your objective is to acquire the skill sets necessary to become a good leader, a better leader in the workplace.

A recent Harvard University study reveals that while most fair-minded managers judge you according to your merits, there are some who judge you according to unconscious stereotypes and attitudes.* It's the kind of prejudice that is not overt. It's prejudice that's subconscious and made through associations that are learned early on. Things commonly associated with each other like thunder and lightning, or gray hair and old age, don't always coexist.

Consequently, being exposed to images and associations like Black men and violence, or Black women and drama, or Black people and

*"How Unethical Are You?" Mahzarin R. Banaji, Max H. Bazerman, and Dolly Chugh, *Harvard Business Review,* 12, 2003.

crime, are associations that play out in the workplace just as they do anywhere else. As a result, be aware that managers who claim not to have a prejudiced bone in their bodies on a conscious level actually believe they are telling the truth. But deep down, they could be operating with these thought processes or associations in mind.

In the Harvard study, subjects who believe they have no negative feelings toward, say, Black Americans or the elderly are nevertheless likely to be *slower* to associate Black faces with "good" words than they are to associate youthful or white faces with "good" words. Also, that "in-group favoritism" is a bias that favors the dominant culture. People tend to do more favors for those they know and those they feel to be like them; people who share their nationality, social class, and perhaps religion, race, employer, or alma mater. With this being the case, when those in the majority or those in power allocate scarce resources (such as jobs and promotions) to people just like them, they effectively discriminate against those who are different from them. This in-group favoritism amounts to giving "extra credit" for group membership. Whereas discriminating against those who are different is considered to be unethical, helping people close to them is often viewed favorably. Invariably, these are attitudes that you may face that you obviously have no control over, but need to be aware of. If it gets in your way, you must see it as one of many hurdles you must climb on your quest for leadership. All the more reason you should go out of your way to be an individual and be recognized for your accomplishments.

Keep in mind managers come from many cultures and that each culture has its own prejudice and bias. Nevertheless, you can't let other people's hang-ups prevent you from reaching your goals. Find a way to ignore, overlook, and overcome as you pursue your quest.

Don't get mad, get knowledge and experience to become the best leader you can possibly be. Turn racism into the rocket fuel that will propel you to the next level.

CULTURAL CODE

Even though we sometimes feel invisible and overlooked in the workplace, we must stay focused and work hard at achieving our goals. It is also because of this pressure that many of us give up in the corporate environment and move on to do other things, like becoming entrepreneurs. No one said the road to leadership would be easy. Look at it this way: We've come this far so we must be doing something right. Racism is not an excuse to do less than our best. But sometimes it can be used as a motivator to keep us moving forward because we want to prove others wrong and do whatever we can to change their thinking. These prejudices may frustrate us and make us angry, but we can channel this energy to make us even more determined to achieve our leadership goals.

MAMAisms

- Just because other people have problems, don't make them yours.
- You can't keep a good sistah down . . . for long.
- Don't get caught up in what other people think.
- No one can make you feel inferior without your consent.
- You are just as good as anybody else.

4

Don't Be the Office Mammy

 trong Black Women: We hear the phrase all the time. But that
 concept can be a double-edged sword. From a cultural stand-
point, many of us assume the role of Rock of Gibraltar, having to in-
tervene in family situations when there's conflict or take on financial
responsibility for a relative whose economic resources are limited.
This reality, compounded with the stereotypical image of the Black
woman as "Mammy," or a self-sacrificing Black woman who takes
care of those around her, can easily shift us into the caregiver role.
As a result, extending this behavior from our families, churches, and
communities becomes a key failure if you transfer this attitude to
the office. Not to be confused with "Be willing to do what others
won't," or refusing to do a task because it's "not your job," or
"rolling up your sleeves and getting your hands dirty," because a
leader's job is to get things done. This is about not volunteering to
become the "mother hen" or servant of your department. Of course
you will assist and encourage others, but you should not do so to the
detriment of your own career and possibly to the detriment of your
own mental and physical health. We can do anything, but we cannot
do everything. So don't put yourself at the bottom of your to-do list.
If you do, others will put you there, too.

CULTURAL CODE

Instead of becoming the resident "caregiver," we should establish ourselves as the resident "specialist" with expertise in specific areas. We can certainly refer people to others to assist them with whatever they may need, but we should refrain from always providing those direct services ourselves. This shift from "mothering" or serving everyone who approaches us to "referring" them to others may take some doing, but the transition, which is a very important one, is definitely worth it in the long run. Trying to care for everyone's needs leaves us open to becoming overworked and overwhelmed and can even lead to depression. Because we may feel responsible for the care of so many others, we may begin to neglect ourselves, feel guilty or embarrassed when we cannot do it all, and fail to ask for help trying to carry the load. We must remember that we have earned the right to our positions and do not need to "pay" for the "privilege" of being in Corporate America by serving others, whether actually or symbolically.

MAMAisms

- ○ You already have the right to be here.
- ○ If you don't put yourself first, you can't help others.
- ○ No one can be a superwoman all the time.
- ○ Everything is not your responsibility.
- ○ You can never change what you allow yourself to tolerate.

Use Your Duality to Build Strength

You build your career in a corporate environment and cultivate personal, spiritual, and leisure time activity within the Black community. Like a chameleon you move seamlessly in both worlds, yet you also have the double burden of having to deal with both racism and sexism.

Living in this world of double burdens leaves you with no choice but to be strong. You must be able to get along with others, and at the same time you must be on your guard. You must know how to play with your peers while at the same time prepare yourself to do battle or compete with them. Make these "burdens" part of a single leadership strategy that will make you stronger, more resilient, and insightful.

It was W. E. B. DuBois who first recognized this sense of duality among Black people, which he wrote about in his classic work, *The Souls of Black Folk*, in 1903. "It is a peculiar sensation, this double-consciousness, the sense of always looking at one's self through the eyes of others . . . one never feels his twoness—an American, a Negro: two souls, two thoughts, two unreconciled strivings; two warring ideals in one dark body, whose dogged strength alone keeps it from being torn asunder."

CULTURAL CODE

Whereas it's easy to get pissed off, frustrated, or just plain give up because we have so many factors coming at us at one time, we must use these dichotomies to give us strength. With all the challenges we face, it makes even our smallest achievement all the more valuable. Because we live in the dominant culture, we know more about others than they know about us. We cross the line into their world all the time, but they may rarely come into ours. This is all the more reason to broaden our thinking; read and learn about what goes on in the world, keep up with current events, pay attention to what makes others tick so we have a better understanding about how others think, feel, and what they might do next. Don't be annoyed by this process; instead learn from it, embrace it, and use this knowledge to your advantage. It's an investment of time that's worth making to get to the next level of leadership.

MAMAisms

- ○ **Life isn't fair.**
- ○ **What doesn't kill you, makes you stronger.**
- ○ **Celebrate your knowledge of the dominant culture and make it work for you.**
- ○ **In this case, being two-faced is not a bad thing.**
- ○ **Make the best of both worlds.**

Acknowledge That There Is a Game and Accept That You Must Play

As children we learn to play games, and at an early age we learn they are fun. As we get older we look forward to playing games at recess, then to structured games at gym class, move on to organized games, sports such as tennis, volleyball, basketball, etc., including card games. All the while we're learning to play these games and getting better at them, our strategy for winning improves, our understanding of the rules becomes more sophisticated, and we still love the objective of these games, which is to win. At work a similar gaming concept applies, although that game is known as the company's culture. As soon as you land a job or start a new one, you are put into play. This happens whether you like it or not. You become a player who gets moved to achieve company goals, or benched where you sit in one spot watching as co-workers or other players pass you by, or moved to the sidelines where you're marginalized—or worse, kicked out of the game altogether, a.k.a. "fired." That's just the way it is. To refuse to play the game would be a big mistake and automatically disqualify you from participating in the leadership arena. Make it your mission to figure out what the game is in your environment, and at your company. Keep in mind "there's no shame in the game."

First and foremost, you need to understand your company's culture. To be a leader, you can't get into a job and think it's the way you want it to be. The culture is not going to change to your way of thinking. Quite the contrary. It works the other way around. You need to understand what the culture is and decide if you want to be a part of it. Don't say, "That's politics. I don't want to know about it," or "I can't be bothered and couldn't care less." You have to pay attention to it, especially if you want to advance. So learn early. Perhaps you're in a corporate culture that's team oriented and everything is done in groups, or you're in a culture where ideas are developed in brainstorming sessions and thrown against the wall, so to speak, in order to see what sticks. Maybe you're in a culture that's highly competitive or extremely hierarchical or conservative, or a culture where you're expected to be vocal and assertive. If you're in a culture that makes you feel uncomfortable, you need to adjust and get over it. The other option is to leave on your own or expect that if others feel you're not fitting in, you may get pushed out.

When you're just starting out in your career, or just starting a new job, that is the time to learn about the culture and pay attention to the politics. At the entry level you should be like a sponge and watch and absorb what's going on. Observe who wins, who loses, and why. You should be aware of what's going on in your environment all the time. Be an "active learner," not a "passive" one. See who gets what they want and how they get it. Learn from other people's mistakes and their achievements. Take notes in your PLN to keep track of how more experienced workers are able to win in various situations. Make keeping track of how successes are accomplished in your department fun, interesting, engaging—make it a game. The lesson here is learn early and get with the culture by watching the other players, especially the ones who are promoted, or find another culture that's better suited to your core values so you don't feel like you're compromising your integrity or selling your soul.

CULTURAL CODE

As adults we may think we're too old to play games. Some of us may even think playing games is not ladylike and choose not to get involved. Others may think games go against our spiritual beliefs and values. We may feel that it's deceptive and we're not being true to ourselves, which makes it difficult to adjust and adapt. But the mistake that many of us make is thinking that we have only to do our job, and work the nine-to-five or long hours with lots of overtime. But we must understand the culture and make it work for us. Well, the truth is, the higher up the ladder you go and the more leadership skills you acquire, the more intense the politics become. So shift your mind-set from "You need to change" to "What can I change?" and "How can I change?" and learn to play the game. Furthermore, when you think of yourself as a player you're more inclined to view yourself objectively and take what comes your way less personally. You see what goes on around you from a different perspective. Learn from all the bumps and bruises and time-outs you get along the way. The more you play the more skills you acquire, and the more staying power and endurance you have. No matter how you slice it, in order to become a leader, you have to be involved. Good leadership requires openness to change. So get in there, hang in there, and do your best.

MAMAisms

- ○ Stay in the game no matter what position you play.
- ○ It's a real world out there. It's not the way you want it to be. It is the way it is.
- ○ You have to be in it to win it.
- ○ Give it all you've got.
- ○ Get on your mark, get set, go!

What You Have to Say Is Just as Important as What Others Have to Say, So Speak Up

Remember, you are a VIP. A VIP's voice is her strength, so it's important for your voice to be heard. Use it with confidence to express your opinions. However, the manner in which you communicate is just as important as what you have to say. Your communication skills will often determine how you will be perceived. Pay attention to your tone, your body language, and even your inflection.

You do not have to let everyone know what you think about *every* issue, but others need to know that you have valid opinions that should be taken seriously. Be positive and confident. Don't think or let others think that they know more than you. Your knowledge and experiences are just as valid as theirs.

Depending upon your work environment, you may be accustomed to a set way of contributing your opinion to project discussions or meetings. What you may not know is that usually there is a "communications culture" already established. The first step is to observe and analyze the "communications culture" in your workplace so that opinions are heard and ideas generated are encouraged and not stifled, ignored, or stolen. Even if you speak up, if you are speaking to the wrong person and/or at the wrong time or place, your idea may not be heard or may be passed over.

Once you understand how ideas are put forward in your workplace, you should use the methods of "speaking up" that make the most sense for you in your particular environment. For example, if you work in a place where your colleagues routinely hold discussions in the hallways outside their offices versus at actual organizational meetings, then you must learn to join in the banter and play along with the group. If, on the other hand, your peers are more formal in the ways they put forward suggestions, and they always submit written proposals with some justifications and data analysis, then you need to learn to parallel their methods.

We were taught to be polite, but manners don't always serve us. Sometimes you can't be as nice as you think you should be or were brought up to be. For example, being in a meeting, you can't always wait your turn to speak. Sometimes you must speak out of turn to make your point or express your opinion. No one is going to invite you to speak, so when there is a pause or lull in the discussion, just jump into the conversation. The last thing you want to do is to sit there swallowing your words because no one gave you a chance or permission to talk.

Also, don't miss opportunities to let people you want to impress hear about what you have accomplished, projects you've worked on, programs you're involved with, or future goals you have. There are ways to do this in general conversations without sounding boastful. For example, share your accomplishments for the department via email to your senior management team so you're able to report on ways you add value to your department, company, or organization without bragging. If each person is expected to have something to say, or present at a meeting, be prepared. Or if people are brainstorming and shouting out ideas, join them and don't sit there being quiet. If you're shy, picture yourself at the Thanksgiving table and speak up just as loudly as you would if you were sitting with your friends and family members.

It rarely hurts to present your ideas through more than one medium, to follow up your spoken contribution to a discussion with an email or short memorandum crystallizing your ideas, so you get full credit for your creative thinking. If you have made a formal presentation including an audiovisual program, send your Power-Point deck, slides, or CD with a short introductory note to your managers, and perhaps others as well, as appropriate.

Practice speaking clearly and passionately rather than emotionally, and then speak up on issues about which you and others care. The way you speak about your ideas are just as important as the ideas themselves. The sound and forms of speech you use are just as important as the message. If you do speak up and others diminish your contributions, don't get discouraged. For example, speak in declarative sentences. Say "I think that this project could work because . . . ," and back up your claim with facts, stories, or examples of successful ideas that have worked and others will take you more seriously. And always remember a positive declaration is more powerful than a negative one.

Don't let others know or see that you're afraid to speak up. They will determine that to be a weakness, and they will stop taking you seriously. Or worse, they may also stop inviting you to important meetings if they don't expect you to participate in a meaningful way. So remember, the more you practice expressing your opinions, the more confident you will become in your ability to assert yourself in a business environment.

CULTURAL CODE

Sometimes we tend to be intimidated by those in the dominant society because they have had many of the advantages and access to opportunities that we have not had. Under these circumstances it's easy to think they know more than we do. However, organizations can benefit from diverse opinions and we may bring a different perspective to the table. Just because we think others have good ideas, we should not suppress our own.

Don't be too shy to speak up in meetings. We must listen to what's being said and jump in with an opinion. Ask valid questions and don't be afraid to share with the group. The best thing we can do for ourselves, our reputation, and credibility, is to have a voice. If advance information is not available, we have to think "on our feet" or "in the moment" as the problem or issue is being presented. Don't worry if what you say turns out to be off point and judged wrong or inappropriate. We may surprise ourselves with our own creativity.

Also, don't be surprised if you have an opinion and you aren't heard. Then seconds later a male counterpart expresses the same sentence, thought, or sentiment and is heard and congratulated on his thinking. It happens often (call it selective hearing). In any case, when this occurs you may want to respond, "Great! I'm glad you agree with me," just to let people know that you had the idea and expressed it first.

 **MAMAisms**

- ○ **Stop mumbling. Open your mouth and speak.**
- ○ **If you've got something to say, say it.**
- ○ **Always have something to say.**
- ○ **Let people know that the lights are on and somebody's home.**
- ○ **Don't let the cat get your tongue.**

Aretha Was Right: R-E-S-P-E-C-T

We all want to be liked, but as VIPs we must do everything possible to be respected; it is respect that will take us farther down the road to leadership. Being liked will attract others to you because you are "nice," whereas being respected makes others acknowledge your competence and skill. By acting like the VIP you truly are, you will command respect in your workplace. Regardless of your position, you need to generate a respectful approach to your work, your co-workers, and your place on the team. Treat everyone as you wish to be treated. You don't have to love them, or even like them, but you do need to respect them and their positions, just as they need to respect you.

What if they don't treat you well despite your best efforts? You must learn to deal with it strategically. Sooner or later they will come off as being the jerk. Whatever you do, you'll be much better off if you don't lose your cool, particularly if to do so will give your manager(s) or colleagues ammunition to use against you. Under the best circumstances, respect will get you noticed. If you're well-liked, too, that's just icing on the cake.

CULTURAL CODE

Sometimes we're afraid to take a stand or a position for fear that we won't be liked. But keep in mind, followers are liked and leaders are respected. Get the picture? Your goal is to be respected. In order to attain respect, you must be willing to take a stand that may be unpopular. Leaders are often tested in this way; however, it's important not to be intimidated by what others may think or to second-guess yourself. On the other hand, it's okay to change your mind after receiving new or better information. A good leader who is open to changing her position with valid reasons can still be respected. When we second-guess ourselves we become paralyzed, we can't make a decision, and we lose respect.

MAMAisms

○ **Stand for something.**
○ **Treat people the way you want to be treated.**
○ **You don't have to be liked to be respected.**
○ **Being popular isn't the only thing that matters.**
○ **Leadership is not synonymous with friendship.**

Listen Up! Understanding What's Said v. What's Meant

Listening—the ability to understand and retain information—is the single most important of all communications skills. It is an art that takes practice, and improving your skills as a listener is one of the very best things you can do as a developing leader. Listening well is hardly ever done these days, especially as we are all pushed to do everything faster, often preparing to speak as someone else is talking because we think we don't have time to do everything else on our agenda.

As a listener, your challenge is to try to hear both what is said and what is meant by the speaker. That discernment may take some time, which is why you must be careful not to respond too quickly or interrupt someone in the middle of listening, unless it is to summarize what is being said in order to reinforce your understanding. A good rule of thumb is to first think about what the person has said before you compose and utter your response. If you can remember what was said accurately, you are becoming an effective listener, and you are more likely to make an appropriate response.

What usually happens is that when someone says glowing things about you or your work, your ears open wide and you hear every word. However, when less positive things are being said, like when someone opposes your views or convictions, or is giving you constructive criticism about your work, you might selectively hear only those fragments of the conversation that make you feel comfortable.

Listening well takes practice, patience, and experience. Work on developing this very important skill. One great way to make sure you've heard a conversation correctly is to "play it back" verbally or in written form for confirmation by the other party(ies) involved. Often a quick summary verbally as in, "This is what I heard you say," or in written form, "Attached is a summary of our conversation, meeting, planning session, etc. . . . Please let me know if you have any corrections or suggestions." Presenting this summary lets others know that you were listening carefully, and gives them the opportunity to give you important feedback if you misunderstood anything that was said.

In fact, listening is so important to leadership advancement that the subject is actually taught at colleges, universities, and management training centers for leaders (including corporate executives, politicians, and managers of nonprofit organizations) in many places around the world. Usually after just one listening exercise, you will be amazed at how much more carefully you listen to people and how much more you remember of what they said.

It's also important to be able to "decode" the physical communications that are being sent along with the words in any conversation. Practice neutral body language and facial expressions, so that your sitting rigidly and/or frowning during a meeting is not misinterpreted as anger, disagreement, or boredom when you may be only concentrating. Similarly, always take note of the other person's facial expressions, tone of voice, and physical posture or gestures while they are speaking, which may give you helpful clues as to how they feel about what they are saying. If the person you are listening to is not looking at you, fidgeting, fumbling with other objects or papers, s/he is likely distracted and not focusing on the subject at hand. Your job in this instance is to listen and ask questions if their intent is unclear or confusing. Remember to try summarizing the meaning or "take away" from the conversation and confirm your understanding with the speaker to make sure you got it right.

Long pauses between words doesn't necessarily mean something negative, as the speaker could be shy or modest or may have even stuttered at an earlier time in his life. There are times, though, when pauses do send their own subtle messages. Interpreting these messages can be tricky, and it helps to have friends (whether in the workplace who may know the speaker or outside of the organization) to assist you in teasing out what the person is really trying to communicate to you.

The place where a conversation is held is often as important as the conversation itself. Often important talks are held in "impromptu" spots, like restrooms, company cafeterias, off-site meetings, cabs, airplanes, and/or hallways, which may catch you off guard. It may be even more critical that you remain alert and listen so you not only hear the words, but don't miss the nonverbal cues that are being sent in these "informal" chats that can help you understand the framing of the message. Never be afraid to ask questions and leave the door open to come back after you have had time to think more about the conversation.

Even when you are listening carefully, you may think that your fellow workers are speaking a language you don't understand. If you are new to your workplace, be sure to ask for a list of acronyms or nomenclature that may be commonly used there, so that you can study it and begin to understand the "lingo" that everyone is speaking. It is still quite common for many managers, particularly male leaders, to outline their business strategies using sports vernacular. Whether or not you care about sports, you do need to be able to decipher what a "full-court press" or a "long pass" may mean in the business context.

CULTURAL CODE

We may think we know what someone is trying to say, particularly if we make assumptions about them and their motives or agendas. But generally speaking, we are not learning when our mouths are moving. We are also not learning when we become too focused on what we want to say, the points we want to make, or when we spend time judging whether or not the person speaking is right or wrong. Pay attention to what is being said. When people in business fail to hear and understand each other, the results can be disastrous. For example, an important deadline can be missed or a key detail can be left out of a report or project and jeopardize its success. Consequently, your reputation as an effective leader can be impaired. It is critically important to take time to listen, no matter how rushed we may feel. By listening effectively we not only learn what others think, but what they are planning to do. We can hear information that is important to doing our jobs effectively and inspire us to develop a plan of action or find other ways to prepare for upcoming opportunities. Listening well can also give us clues about subtle or major changes that may be occurring in our departments or companies that we should know about. We should always be engaged in this "active listening." When we listen attentively and patiently, we will be well on our way to becoming more effective leaders.

 ## MAMAisms

- ○ You can't hear what I'm saying when you're talking over me.
- ○ Look at me when I'm talking to you!
- ○ Don't make me repeat myself.
- ○ Pay attention to what I'm saying to you.
- ○ How many times do I have to tell you?

10

Always Have a Plan of Action and Follow Through

To be a successful leader you must set goals and objectives and adjust them as the circumstances require, and never lose sight of where you're headed. Goals—both personal and professional—give you something to strive for. They keep you focused. They allow you to measure your success. So start out by setting small goals and build to setting goals that are challenging but also realistic, goals that are clear and measurable, and short-term and long-term goals.

In order to stay on track with your goals, make an action plan. Take a sheet of paper and draw two lines from top to bottom, creating three columns. On the far left, write down all the things you want to accomplish this year. Just write down whatever makes sense for you in your current position to help you get to where you want to be in the near future. In your PLN write things down in no particular order. For example:

- I want to come up with three new strategies for my team to achieve its goals this year.
- I'm going to get feedback from my boss upon completion of every project.
- I want to exercise to stay in shape to look better and feel better.
- I want to add to my wardrobe to begin to dress like I already have my next job.

- I will write down the results of my accomplishments at the end of every month.
- I will take a time-management class to help improve my performance.

Whatever your goals are, write them down. In the middle column, put a number next to each goal in order of priority. In the right column, list the approximate time frame for achieving these goals, such as spring, or by my birthday, or by the end of the third quarter, etc. This document then becomes your action plan.

When you reach one goal, reward yourself. Then move on to the next goal, feeling empowered by what you've already achieved. Setting goals not only helps you get to where you want to go, but it also makes your self-confidence grow even more. That's the way it works. Set little goals. Meet them. Set new, slightly larger goals. Meet them. Succeed. Sometimes you succeed on schedule, sometimes things will take longer to achieve than you thought, sometimes your goals will change. The point is to keep planning and plugging away to move forward.

CULTURAL CODE

It's important to find the discipline to keep a record of all that we do. It's the only way we grow and advance to the next level. If we take what we do for granted, then others will too, and then we wonder why we're stuck in the same position doing the same thing. Since your goal is leadership, your action plan is an important tool. **So no excuses.** Start creating one today. At the end of every day, week, or month, whatever makes sense to you, write down your accomplishments and compare them to the goals you have set for yourself. If you feel you need to add in smaller goals to reach the larger goals, then do so, but stay on track.

 **MAMAisms**

○ There's no time like the present.
○ You don't get any dessert until you eat all your food.
○ Don't put off until tomorrow what you can do today.
○ Plan your work and work your plan!
○ Don't just talk about it, do it!

Don't Let Your Emotions Get the Best of You

xercising self-control over your feelings is just as important as mastering the skills of your job. There's a term for this: Emotional Intelligence—and it's not taught in schools; it's a life skill, and something you'll be evaluated on at the office whether you know it or not. Emotional Intelligence has to do with how you manage yourself and your relationships. You've heard of IQ—the Intelligence Quotient. Well, EI is all about interpersonal effectiveness, including how you handle or react to various situations, especially those that tend not to be in your favor.

You have all faced challenging situations in your lives and sometimes these tests occur in the workplace. Although it may be hard to imagine when you are going through a difficult situation, it is true that lessons can be learned from every experience that you encounter. It is with this in mind that you should reevaluate your perception of tough times at work and view them as opportunities to learn.

In other words, challenges are sometimes just the kick you need to recharge, renew, and reinvent.

Instead of jumping to conclusions, cursing someone out, throwing a fit, or slamming the door to your office, listen to what is being said, or examine what is happening and sleep on it before you respond. Get angry someplace else, not at work. Take a step back and give yourself twenty-four hours to cool down. Sound off in a letter, but don't send it. Go to the gym after work and get on a treadmill. Getting angry to the point where others in the office become aware of it, may cause you to say something you'll regret, which of course, isn't a smart thing to do. In fact, it's a huge mistake that can potentially jeopardize your current position as well as prevent your advancement.

In most cases, you have a negative reaction to situations that you view as difficult or unfair. Emotions would have you think that you are protecting yourself and leveling the playing field. The problem, however, may be that the way in which you react can put more of a disparaging light on you than on the situation. Rather than letting your emotions drive you, think about what you will gain or lose from your reaction. "Think" is the operative word here. Know there are several ways to look at a situation and that it's better to think things through before you react. In other words, it's more important to be levelheaded than to prove you are right. Ask yourself the following questions: What are the choices I can make? What would I like the end result to be? What strategic moves can I make to get the outcome that I want? Oftentimes you can turn the situation around when you react in a nonemotional and strategic way. Learning to utilize the four areas of Emotional Intelligence can be of great benefit to you in this regard:

- *self-awareness:* Acknowledge the problem and how it is affecting you. Learn to understand your emotions and evaluate your tendencies during these difficult or challenging situations.
- *self-management:* Develop a strategic plan to get what you need. What do you want to happen if you act or do not react to the situation?
- *social awareness:* How might the situation look to the other person involved? Think about and try to identify what is really going on with the other person.

• *relationship management:* Show flexibility to get results. Use your understanding of the other three emotional intelligence skills to manage interactions.

Each one of these skills can be learned with practice and can be utilized throughout your career.

Emotional Intelligence is being aware of your emotions and those of others. Your objective is to preserve relationships, not to create adversaries. Emotional Intelligence allows you to take your game to the next level. You become the one in control when you can manage your emotions and do not let people or situations keep you from accomplishing the career success you deserve. You need a high degree of EI in order to become an effective leader.

CULTURAL CODE

When things don't go our way some of us tend toward anger, which is a negative emotion. We might get pissed off and tell people where to go, finger-point, do the neck-rolling thing, and turn into the Angry Black Woman. Perhaps we might hold in the anger and disappointment and suffer in silence. Some may react by blaming others and passing judgment, which makes people get defensive. By taking time to identify our feelings and consider our reactions we can respond more effectively. Do your research on the issue to understand why certain decisions were made, even if you think you already know. If you find out it was because you didn't have the right skills, then get the right training. If it was because of a change in the corporate mission, then you know you have no control over that and can't take it personally. Monitor and adapt your own emotions and behaviors for the benefit of yourself, your team, and your department. Don't automatically feel defeated or paranoid that others are out to get you. It is not an automatic sign of defeat to not react to a challenging situation but rather a sign of emotional maturity. Always stick to the facts and make sure you have the right information before you react. Be smart in more ways than one. If you don't manage your emotions, you have to do damage control if you explode. You may find that the only thing to do is to suck it up and apologize directly for your emotional outburst. You're allowed only a few of these incidents before you get labeled the Angry Black Woman, which is a far cry from the successful Black leader that you're striving to be.

 **MAMAisms**

- He who angers you, controls you.
- Don't say anything until you hear the whole story.
- Let it go like water rolling off the back of a duck.
- Never let them see you sweat.
- It is better to sleep on things beforehand than to lie awake about them afterward.

Developing Good Relationships With Co-Workers Has More Benefits Than You Think

One of the prerequisites for becoming a good leader is to like people. You cannot be a truly effective leader, the kind that people want to follow, unless you care about others, have their best interests in mind, and understand how they think and feel. If your relational skills are weak, your leadership will always suffer. To improve your relationships you must:

- Get the focus off yourself and care about others.
- Smile at people, whether they are senior executives, receptionists, or work in the mail room.
- Make others feel special. Call them by name. You never know if you may need them: The person in the other department may become your boss or sponsor one day or may be the person who recommends you for a promotion or new position.
- Show interest in people, share common ground and experiences; include them, (but don't tell them all your business).
- Give someone an unexpected gift; something you make, bake, or buy.
- Make time to chitchat around the office watercooler, kitchen area, elevator, or cafeteria (but don't gossip).
- Know that good relationships involve more than just cooperation, but also humor, playfulness, exploration into the world, and time.

- Understand that maintaining a good relationship is easier than repairing one.

CULTURAL CODE

We tend to stick with people who look like us and feel uncomfortable around those who are culturally different. We are also inclined to befriend others who may be the same gender or age because that's what feels safe. Challenge yourself to expand your circle of colleagues. Broaden the spectrum of your relationships. Being cliquish doesn't work to our advantage. It doesn't increase our universe or help us expand our learning. Save the cliquish behavior for personal friendships. In the workplace the key is to be a people person, since as a leader you'll have to represent, influence, problem-solve, communicate, and in general connect with people in many ways on many different levels.

 ## MAMAISMS

- ○ It's not what you know, but who you know.
- ○ Keep your friends close and your enemies closer.
- ○ Always try to see the good in people.
- ○ The same people you see going up, you see coming back down.
- ○ You can catch more flies with honey than you can with vinegar.

Communicate Clearly in Person and on Paper

No matter what your job is, you must make time to communicate and do it well. Communication is both a skill and an art. Even though you've been communicating all your life, effective communication is a whole different animal. People will judge your intelligence by the way you speak. For example, whether you pronounce the letter "g" at the end of your verbs may let others consciously or subconsciously draw conclusions about your level of education, despite the fact that you may have a college degree. For example, you need to check whether you say "goin'" instead of "going," or "axe" instead of "ask." It doesn't matter if others say it in the office, *you* can't. One of the first things you need to do is make sure you have a handle on your grammar. Using correct sentence structure at all times, enunciating your words, increasing your vocabulary, and improving your mastery of the English language is the only way you'll get your ideas understood and have others listen. Having the ability to communicate is the only way leaders get people to follow.

You'll need effective communication skills to inspire, persuade, influence, and motivate others. You'll need these skills to make various presentations, pitch ideas for marketing campaigns, deliver facts that support your work, or when you're ready to ask for a raise or make a case for your promotion.

Written communication is just as important. In this world of business communication and electronic mail, most company communications are done in writing. You must know how to write. And if you're insecure about your writing skills, you must learn by any means necessary. There are adult classes, night school at community colleges, universities, online classes, and books to guide you. You want to practice both verbal and written communication at this point in your career, so you'll be prepared for the opportunities that come your way.

Nonverbal communication is to be taken seriously as well. What you don't say speaks volumes about you. Stand up straight. It signals self-confidence. Be sure to make eye contact with the person you're addressing. If there is more than one person in the room, then this applies to everyone. Use hand gestures in a meaningful way. Don't fidget or appear nervous. Make sure your voice conveys confidence and control. Speak up and speak clearly. Just as important, watch your tone, and always come across as friendly.

Here are some exercises to help you along:

- Write a speech and practice delivering it in the mirror. Look at your body language, eyes, neck, and hands.
- Listen to your voice on a tape recorder. How do you sound? Would you believe you? Would you trust you?
- Visualize yourself speaking to a group.
- Make a presentation using examples to support your claim. Take yourself through an actual demonstration or idea pitch.
- If you're nervous, stay focused and keep breathing.
- Take a class to help you with your presentation skills. Perhaps your company would even pay for this training—for example: Toastmasters.
- Like anything else, the more you practice, the better you'll become.

CULTURAL CODE

Some of us may have grown up hearing proper English being referred to as "talking white," which was always used in a derogatory and accusatory way. There are many among us who were teased because of "talking white" and adopted not talking white as a way of fitting in. The First Lady, Michelle Obama, tells students to aim high and credits her success in part to her command of the English language. "I remember there were kids around my neighborhood who would say, 'Ooh, you talk funny. You talk like a white girl.' I heard that growing up my whole life. I thought, 'I don't even know what that means, but I am still getting my A.'"

Obviously, improper communication is not going to cut it in the corporate world or in any environment where there's opportunity for advancement. Many of us didn't have the advantage of going to prep or private schools at the elementary stages where the basic skills of grammar and communication are taught. To take it a step back, it wasn't that long ago that the *Brown v. Board of Education* decision attempted to make education in the classroom equal. Language is learned at home first, then at school. But if your parents or grandparents didn't receive the best education, or have access to it, then it's up to you to do the work to claim it for yourself. There should be no embarrassment about brushing up on these skills and keeping a dictionary handy in your desk drawer just in case you need it. Also know how to use the dictionary and thesaurus on your computer. If you've already mastered the basics, know there are different formulas for various types of communication. For example, there is a specific way of organizing your thinking to make a sales presentation that may be different than making a creative pitch to present a marketing campaign idea. There is a different way to write copy for advertising than for writing a press release. Find out the writing style that applies to your department and/or company, and learn how to use it to communicate your ideas, express your opinions, and make your points. For whatever industry you're in, there's a style of communication that you must study, learn, and practice.

 **MAMAisms**

○ **Speak like a lady.**
○ **Use proper speech for proper times.**
○ **Choose your words carefully.**
○ **E-nun-ci-ate.**
○ **Speak as if you're already in charge.**

Know Your Value

Don't confuse your net worth with your self-worth. Your net worth is determined by your assets and resources. Your self-worth is determined by your level of self-confidence and the value you have to offer. When it comes to your organization, knowing your self-worth is important. This is when your PLN definitely comes in handy. No matter how big or small, take account of all your accomplishments and write them down. Each time you do something worthy, write it down or else you won't give yourself credit. Keep in mind that if you don't give yourself credit, no one else will, and that's for sure. You need to know what you've done and not depend on other people, including your boss, to keep track of these things for you. This is your responsibility. Knowing how you spend your time is valuable. You need to know what it is that you're doing and why it matters to the company. You need to justify yourself and why you're getting paid to do that job. Because you're busy, the tendency is to forget to write things down, or worse, take the skills you have for granted. And the last thing you want to do is take yourself for granted. But keeping track of these details is exactly the kind of documentation you'll need to articulate your skills and contributions to the company and to use as leverage to negotiate more responsibility and more money. So when you ask for a raise, you'll need to be able to point to at least five contributions that you have made to the company. For example, you'll want to state how you saved the company money, came up with a new idea that changed the way your department does business, what projects you've completed successfully on deadline and under budget, or what new accounts you brought into the company or sales expectations you exceeded. You also need to keep account of year-to-year or month-to-month accomplishments to evaluate your skill sets past and present. This is how you determine your value and self-worth.

To add value to your position you may consider what you do in your outside activities as well. Are you a church leader, volunteer hospital worker, community organizer, block association officer, or committee head of your sorority or social group? Also consider any nonprofit position you hold, to see what skills may transfer to your job. It's quite possible your boss may see your extracurricular activities as assets that can increase your responsibilities at work.

CULTURAL CODE

In general, we tend not to pay attention to our accomplishments. We tend to take ourselves for granted because we know how to do our jobs. But the truth is, we can't lose sight of the skill sets we bring to work every day. Because much of what we do comes naturally to us, we may not necessarily equate it with a specialty or skill. But we should assess what we do professionally and personally and write down all that we've accomplished, and continue to do so on a regular basis. We may be amazed to see how golden we are. The other thing we need to consider is our outside work. For example, many of us are leaders in church. We manage projects, people, build teams, oversee committees, are responsible for balancing budgets and work flow but we may not think about these actions and responsibilities as skill sets. You should be able to look at your skills outside and inside the work arena to know your value and self-worth. Mention your outside skills to your boss and who knows, you may be perceived differently, and when there is an opportunity or an available position at a higher level, you may be considered for it.

 **MAMAisms:**

○ Don't be afraid to stand tall and stick out your chest.
○ You're worth more to me than the whole wide world.
○ Always be prepared.
○ Your self-worth is more important than your net worth.
○ You are worth more than your weight in gold.

To Measure Your Performance, Get Feedback

You may think you're doing a fabulous job and you probably are, but you'll need to get confirmation from the person who matters most, the one who reviews your performance, and is qualified to give you a raise, bonus, or promotion: your boss. Feedback helps you grow, develop, and gives you a chance to correct your mistakes. You're fortunate if you work for a company that gives feedback and reviews on a regular basis. If you don't, you'll have to be proactive and ask for it. Giving feedback makes some managers feel uncomfortable because they don't like to deliver negative news. They think giving negative news is an instigator for interpersonal conflict instead of growth, feel uneasy about the process in general, or simply don't know how to approach this task. But feedback is information that measures how well you achieve your work objectives and results. So when you have your feedback meeting, don't rely on memory. Review the notes of your contributions that you've been tracking in your PLN. Use the information to prepare for this meeting. During the meeting ask relevant questions about your work and seek guidance. It's also the time when your good listening skills come into play. Be sure to take notes on your feedback and most important, don't take negative feedback personally. Remember this is about your performance, not personal criticism. And if you receive constructive criticism, which you will because nobody is perfect, know that these are areas for improvement that simply require more of your time, energy, focus, and attention to develop a better you.

So that you continue to get the feedback you need, ask for it regularly; perhaps quarterly or semi-annually as the case may be, but definitely after the completion of a big project while it's still fresh on your manager's mind.

Of course not all feedback is negative. Positive feedback should give you reassurance that you're moving in the right direction and you should keep up the great work.

CULTURAL CODE

We tend to assume that when we show up for work, do a good job, even stay late, the fact that we're operating on all eight cylinders means that we're right on track. However, there are times when this could not be further from the truth. Just because your boss is not criticizing your work or reprimanding you for not doing a good job doesn't mean he doesn't think that way every now and then. It's your responsibility not to make any assumptions about your overall performance. It's your boss's job to tell you how you're doing. Consequently, even if she feels uneasy about giving you feedback, it's something you must ask her to do. In addition to this, be open to hearing honest feedback from your co-workers and others you interact with on a regular basis as well. As your boss begins to recognize your performance change and see your growth (which you may have to bring to her attention), she'll see you as someone who takes the performance feedback seriously, which is a good way to get noticed and rewarded.

On the other hand, sometimes we sabotage ourselves by ignoring constructive criticism and refusing to change. Other times, we get an attitude and internalize these feelings, which block us from moving forward, and being stuck prevents us from growing. In general, be open to feedback, use it as an opportunity for self-evaluation, and make appropriate changes to your behavior and/or performance if necessary.

 **MAMAisms**

- ○ **Always do your best and don't settle for less.**
- ○ **You can't change what you don't know.**
- ○ **Don't get stuck in the mud.**
- ○ **Never miss an opportunity to learn something new about yourself.**
- ○ **Don't take it personally.**

16

Perception: It's Not Only about How You See Yourself

Once you settle into your position, establish routines and relationships, take a step back and look outside yourself, as if you're having an out-of-body experience. Try to see yourself the way others may see you. How would others describe you? What would they think of you? What is their perception of you? What people perceive is what they usually believe. So reality is not just what you think of yourself, but also what others may think of you as well.

In the arena of leadership, perception, no matter if it's right or wrong to you, is reality to those who perceive you. The fact that people can perceive the same thing differently puts the pressure on you to make sure you project and reinforce a positive perception and change a negative one.

Many organizations provide and offer 360-degree feedback surveys so you can get a sense of how others perceive you. This is when your team, boss, and co-workers answer questions about your performance and rate your effectiveness as a leader, manager, or employee. If you don't have access to 360-degree feedback surveys, you may want to do an informal testing of the people you work with. Ask them what they perceive about you, or what they believe about you, to gain knowledge of yourself and take away their truths, if in fact they are comfortable enough to give you honest and constructive criticism. Open and honest communication can shed valuable insights into your performance and behaviors. If you find there are a few issues or areas that need improvement, pick one or two things to focus on first and work on improving them.

Do others see you as the kind of person who is lazy and pessimistic, disorganized, a loner, or inflexible, or do others see you as someone who comes to work energized, is detail-oriented, is a team player, a strategic or big-picture thinker, and is someone who is compassionate and understanding?

Perception is the process by which people select and gather sensory information to create a meaningful, rational picture of the world around them. You want to make sure that others' perception of you is a positive one. What people think of you will determine whether they will follow you.

CULTURAL CODE

Sometimes we are so comfortable in our jobs because we know what we're doing and we're really good at it, that we overlook what others may think of us. In addition to this, sometimes we may feel what others think of us is unimportant as long as we're doing great work. But what others think is critical to our learning more about ourselves and to becoming good leaders. There's a school of thought that "perception is reality." Whether it's true or not, it's something we need to pay attention to. We should check in every now and then, take a glimpse of ourselves from the outside-in and be open to opportunities for self-improvement. Leaders are constantly learning.

MAMAisms

○ Look in the mirror and see a reflection of your true self.

○ Don't lie to others and don't lie to yourself.

○ Perception is reality.

○ Nobody is perfect, but work on your imperfections.

○ It's easier to look outward than inward.

Seek Guidance and Support

No one becomes successful all by themselves. We benefit from the help of others who have more experience and knowledge and are willing to offer guidance, feedback, and support. Mentors, sponsors, and personal boards of directors can do just that and you should seek to benefit from all of them during your professional career.

A mentor is a trusted adviser, someone you have established a relationship with and from whom you can seek advice. Mentors—yes, you can have more than one—can provide you with words of wisdom to help you navigate through a host of issues that you will encounter during your career. They can be someone within or outside of your organization or in another industry, and they usually offer different perspectives that allow you to make better decisions regarding the issue at hand.

Although many expect their mentors to look like them, you should also be open to individuals who are a different race and/or gender. The upside of this is that it can broaden your horizon and point of view by diversifying your thought process. Having different perspectives allows you to make better decisions in your position as a leader.

A mentor should be a role model, someone who has values and behaviors you wish to emulate. Whether you pick a mentor or a mentor picks you, one thing is for certain: You will usually advance further, faster, and less painfully with a mentor in your life to help you navigate in your career.

Many organizations and industry groups have formal mentor programs. If you belong to an organization that offers one, sign up immediately to be a mentee or a mentor. Organized mentor programs allow you to gain exposure, meet and learn from others, and help you to bring others along. Remember that a mentor-mentee relationship is a two-way street. You give support and guidance and you get it in return.

A sponsor, on the other hand, is an individual who is influential and powerful and can have more impact than a mentor. A sponsor has the ability to get you the exposure needed to advance. This person of influence has the ear of other influential people and brings your accomplishments to the attention of others in the company who also have the power to advance your career. Whereas you know your mentor and you seek advice from him/her, you may not ever know the person who is acting as your sponsor. This individual is going to "talk you up" and help form others' opinion of you, or if necessary, change others' opinion of you. Your sponsors will sing your praises even when you are not around. They're like the "man behind the curtain" whom you never see, but is the one who makes things happen.

Then there is your *personal board of directors* or your *success team*. This is a group of individuals who may or may not know one another but who know you from a variety of perspectives and can help you navigate to reach specific goals. They are trusted advisers who you reach out to because you value their opinion, their objectivity, their knowledge and experience in your specific area of interest or need. They, like mentors, offer advice and feedback, though usually in a specific area of expertise. The individuals on your personal board of directors will vary based on your objectives but may include trusted friends or relatives and/or professional advisers such as an attorney, accountant, or career coach.

CULTURAL CODE

None of us can find success all on our own. We should not be too proud to ask for guidance from those we trust. If we do not have trusted advisers in our life, we should make it our business to seek them out. It takes support and guidance to help us navigate the corporate landscape and we should not be shy about reaching out to use every opportunity available to us.

MAMAisms

- ○ Seek wisdom from your elders.
- ○ It takes a village to raise a child.
- ○ Don't be afraid to reach out.
- ○ If you need help, don't be afraid to ask.
- ○ Two heads are better than one.

Surround Yourself with the Right People: You Cannot Survive in Isolation

lways surround yourself with smart, confident, and positive people. These are the kinds of people who think they can do anything—the "super crowd," the "movers and shakers," the folks who are doing things and going places, the people who are "about something," the go-getters. And if among these folks, you can align yourself with those who will support you through good times and bad times, through sunny days as well as the storms, congratulations! You now have additional people to add to your success team. This doesn't mean that people have to necessarily agree with you and validate your point of view, but rather they can help you gain a broader perspective by presenting a look at the upside and the downside, considering other options and bringing new information into the picture. The right people can come from professional associations, alumni groups, clubs, and personal interest organizations. They can help you gain new perspectives that allow you to advance in your career. And they don't have to be the same people all the time. They don't have to be the same race, gender, age-range, or religion as you. But you do need to have your success team in place to go to for help, guidance, or just to listen. Surrounding yourself with the right people will always be beneficial.

CULTURAL CODE

We're so used to running ourselves into the ground that we think we have to do it all alone. Nothing is farther from the truth. We need to surround ourselves with positive people. With this being said, we also need to let negative people go, even if they've been longtime friends. In order to survive and thrive in the work environment along the road to becoming a leader you need to develop a group of people you can trust for different needs: one person for guidance, one who tells you about networking events, one who listens to you while you vent, one who is a cheerleader in your corner, one who shares insights about the industry you're in. You pick your team of positive supporters and remember two things:

- Always know that the members can rotate in and out.
- Always keep the door open so new members are welcomed on your *success team* at any time.

MAMAisms

- ◯ **God didn't make us to be by ourselves.**
- ◯ **You are who you surround yourself with.**
- ◯ **Don't let other people bring you down.**
- ◯ **No woman is an island. No woman stands alone.**
- ◯ **If you lie down with dogs, you get up with fleas.**

Step Outside Your Comfort Zone

To become a leader, you must step outside your comfort zone. In order to reach people, inspire and motivate them, you must first be able to connect with them. Since this is the case, you must associate with others. Invite colleagues out for a cocktail or coffee after work, or go out to dinner or a movie. Just because your co-workers may not look like you or come from the same culture or background as you, doesn't mean you can't shift your thinking and begin to be open to new experiences. If others go out after work and don't invite you along, ask if it's okay to invite yourself. Chances are they won't say no. Getting to know people and establishing relationships are key to creating your team-building skills and helping you to become the leader you aspire to be. After all, if your goal is to lead your co-workers, know that your followers will be diverse, even if it's only in their thinking. In fact, there is no such thing as a leader who doesn't step outside her comfort zone and take prudent risks. Successful leaders are open to new knowledge and experiences of all kinds. They have to feel comfortable in various situations. Stepping outside your comfort zone applies to socializing as well as to the way you approach your work. Volunteer at the office and do something you've never done before. Accept demanding assignments; you learn much more from them than you do the easy ones. This takes some courage because the outcome may not be as good, but at least it demonstrates that you're interested in your own development. It also prepares you for difficult challenges in the future. And don't be afraid to fail. You only fail if you don't try. See volunteering as an opportunity to examine what's being done in your office versus what's not being done and then take the initiative to do it. Get your boss to notice. If there's not an actual suggestion box at work, act like there is one. Be proactive. You have to do things that you may not consider to be part of your normal job responsibilities, but it's all a part of acquiring new skills and moving to the next level.

CULTURAL CODE

Familiar surroundings make us feel "safe." However, we need to step outside our comfort zone more often, regardless of how uncomfortable it makes us feel or how scary it is. It takes courage, but that's exactly the stuff good leaders are made of; that's exactly what makes us grow. Stepping outside our comfort zone is both external and internal: external in the sense that we need to feel more comfortable with people who may not share our same experiences or backgrounds and venture outside the office with them under social and professional circumstances; internal in the sense that we need to volunteer to do things in the office environment that extend beyond our normal role and responsibilities, like volunteering to be on a task force, help organize a health day at your job, or be fire drill captain. Don't wait for someone else to come along—you be the person who tries something new and steps up to the plate. People who remain engaged in life consistently display an attitude of openness to new and unexpected experiences. They also tend to be good in crises because they are open to seeing opportunity in even the most dire situations.

MAMAisms

○ Don't be afraid to try something new.

○ Don't get stuck doing the same ole thing the same ole way.

○ Stick your toes into the deep end of the pool.

○ Make that leap.

○ Try it, you might like it.

Regardless of Your Position,
Learn about Your Department,
Your Company, and Your Industry

There are many people who suffer from the Ostrich Syndrome: having their head so far in the sand that they focus *only* on the job they are doing. You have to learn about your job, what's going on around you, in your department, your company, and your industry in order to become well-rounded, knowledgeable, and successful. Not only will it make you more knowledgeable and interesting, but also what happens in the world affects what happens in the marketplace and to your competition, and eventually to you. Expanding your knowledge will help you to do a better job and be more creative in coming up with solutions to problems or new ideas to do your work more efficiently or make recommendations that will have value for your department. As you make these kinds of contributions, you begin to take on more of a leadership role. So it's wise to stay current with what's going on in your department, company, and industry, and with the business world in general.

CULTURAL CODE

We tend to stay focused on our job and our paycheck when we should become familiar with all aspects of the industry we work in. It's a huge mistake to be limited and not expand our knowledge, to ignore what's going on around us and not understand how external forces impact and influence what we do. Then we get broadsided if we don't get promoted because we're only focused on our job description. But becoming a leader requires so much more. If you want to get ahead, others need to be aware of all your talents and skills; that includes your broad knowledge and ability to think outside of the box. Subscribe to the *Harvard Business Review*, read the Business section of *The New York Times*, *Business Week*, and other business journals. Join industry organizations and read the trades that report on your industry. This will help you to understand how all the pieces work and begin to put them together. It's information that will give you something to talk about in meetings or around the watercooler or cafeteria, or the topic you talk about with co-workers when you step outside your comfort zone.

 **M A M A ɪ s ᴍ s**

○ **Learn everything you can. Knowledge is power.**
○ **To be competitive, you've got to do your homework.**
○ **The more you know, the better you get.**
○ **Don't limit yourself to your own backyard.**
○ **Whatever you do, be the best.**

21

Entitlement: Nobody Owes You Anything

Sometimes you may feel that just because you are Black and a woman, you have suffered enough and you deserve to have what you want and have it now. We understand that feeling. Especially when you watch while others, usually, but not always, white and male, seem to sail through their careers and become great successes while you are "slaving" away for "crumbs from the corporate table." There is a concept called "white privilege" that refers to the members of the dominant culture in our society not having to learn about the cultural differences and strengths of the nondominant members of the culture, while those nondominant members (meaning us) have to master the language, cultural mores, interests, and skill sets of the dominant culture in order to be successful, while also remaining connected to our own very distinctive cultures. So as a Black woman you may feel you have to be multicultural, multilingual, and multifaceted and yet keep yourselves fully integrated so that you can function seamlessly in any setting you find yourselves. Often you are so used to operating in this way that you're not aware of the many shifts you make to communicate effectively and efficiently in different circumstances. But sometimes, especially if you are working very hard and competitively, it can be exhausting to have to be aware of so many different things at once, when it seems that your "competition" may be able to stay focused only on his or her career.

Some young women of color seem to feel that they already "have it made," because they were able to go to certain schools and/or grow up in certain communities. They don't seek guidance from more senior women executives in their workplaces or participate in company mentoring programs or career development training sessions because they think they already know what they need to know to get ahead. While this may be true for a few of you, far more of you grow discouraged as you toil away, not talking to anyone and not seeking feedback from your managers, peers, or even your friends or family members, because you think you must do it all yourselves. Some of you may have grown up in a very comfortable environment because your families were able to afford certain advantages for you. Be blessed and grateful for that, but don't expect that just because of it you will automatically be skipped over everyone else who has worked just as hard as you have to be made the new "star" on your job. It's probably not going to happen, and that's going to have to be OK with you, at least for a while. The idea that "you exist, therefore you deserve" is not a sound one, and it's not going to get you very far in the workplace although it may work for you at home.

On the other hand, some of you don't think you'll ever make it, because no matter how hard you try, you can't seem to get a chance to move forward or catch the ear of your supervisor. You're doubtful about your abilities and lack confidence in yourself, although you're obviously smart and capable. You may spend a lot of time worrying and complaining, and too often "whine" your way out of your job while you tattle on everyone else: "So-and-so has only been here three months and *she* got a promotion, why can't I get one?" or "I know the manager doesn't like me, but he sure likes so-and-so and *that's* why he moved up ahead of me." Some of you may be working hard but not "smart," and not learning from your experiences or your environment so that you can map out a strategy for moving forward. Just because you are working very, very hard you are not guaranteed to advance, and your "sweat equity" may not always move the needle in your quest for leadership positions.

No matter when or where you were born, you probably have learned about the injustices Black people and women in general faced in this country (and others in the world), or maybe you have even faced some of those injustices yourself. Regardless of how painful your experiences have been, in order to become a capable and strong leader, you're going to have to get over them and find ways to move forward without being angry or bitter. You certainly need to be aware of racism that can be very direct or very subtle in the workplace, but you cannot let it get you down.

You should not spend so much time feeling *entitled* to better treatment, for any reason, that you fail to take every opportunity to put your best foot forward by being a team player, performing every work responsibility promptly and efficiently, volunteering to take on new challenges, and seeking out information and training from others (no matter what they look like) who can help you. No matter what the past has been and no matter how talented and smart you are now, you're not automatically *entitled* to become a leader at your job, or to even have or keep your current position. Although you may owe a huge debt to your parents, teachers, or community and civil rights leaders, the truth is that nobody owes *you* anything. You have to work! So get to it.

The best leaders earn their place in the world and demonstrate on a daily basis their leadership skills and experience. They don't believe they are automatically entitled to their status or position because of any past experience or injustice, and usually spend their time focused on how to move themselves and the people they are leading forward. Learn from them.

CULTURAL CODE

From centuries of being denied equal access to education and employment, we may feel a sense of entitlement based on the notion that we have to "make up" for all those lost years when people who looked like us were treated so unfairly. For example, after the Civil War, each freed slave was supposed to receive forty acres and a mule, as decreed by General William Sherman, but that decree was later rescinded by President Andrew Jackson. Many historians and civil rights advocates believe this failure to distribute land to slaves so that they could become self-sufficient is the root of the economic disparities of wealth that continue in our country today.* No matter what we may think about these historical theories, in the modern workplace we are still not *entitled* to anything.

Think about it. If we believe that we're *entitled* to certain rights and privileges without working for them, we may just wait and wait and not plan or grow our skill sets and consequently, we will not progress. We can become embittered and unhappy while we are not progressing. We also give away our power to improve our work situations by waiting for the entitlements we have decided we deserve.

We must strategize and become responsible for ourselves, steadily increasing our responsibilities and seeking or creating opportunities for advancement. In doing so, we can use our sense of *entitlement* to motivate us in our quest for leadership success.

---

*"40 Acres and a Mule," BlackHistory.com.
"40 Acres and a Mule," Wikipedia.
"White Privilege: Unpacking the Invisible Knapsack," by Peggy McIntosh.

 **MAMA**ısms

○ God bless the child who has her own.

○ You have to earn what you get to really appreciate it.

○ You're responsible for you.

○ There is no elevator to success; you have to take the stairs.

○ Let the work you've done speak for you.

The Values You Were Raised with in Church Aren't Always Valued in Business

Do unto others as you would have them do unto you.
Thou shalt not steal.
Thou shalt not bear false witness against thy neighbor.
Turn the other cheek.

The Golden Rule, The Ten Commandments, and other parables and teachings from the Bible are among the values some of us grew up with in church. And you don't have to be Christian to share these basic principles. But what are the proper parameters of religious beliefs in deciding what's right for oneself in the business environment and in respecting what's right for the corporation as a whole?

In general, it's in the company's best interest to be ethical because it's important to its function as an organization, to its integrity, its reputation in the marketplace, its ability to attract and retain the best and the brightest employees, and to be competitive and maintain its standing in the community. But don't get it twisted: The ethics of business are different from the ethics of religion.

If you accept that navigating a corporate environment is a "game," the nature of "game" automatically calls for competition and distrust of the other players. After all, the object of the game is to win. Subsequently, you are not in the game with your friends, but rather opponents, and as in poker or bid whist, there are times when you must conceal your own strengths, knowledge, and intentions. Bending the rules, using them to your advantage, manipulating the truth, exaggerating a story, inflating the numbers—these are the rules of the game, the standards of right and wrong that differ from what you learn in Sunday school or from the pulpit on Sunday mornings. Similarly, a mother's message to "be nice" or "forgive and forget" (in business you should forgive, but never forget), can have benefits in your personal life, but have negative consequences for you at work as you pursue your leadership position.

Biblical principles sometimes collide with business ethics. For example, telling the truth, the whole truth, and nothing but the truth, may translate in the business world as "telling the half-truth," "withholding the whole truth," or telling the little white lie—making up a "new truth" for the sake of a better business strategy, solution, or result. In business telling the whole truth could mean missing an opportunity to make a killing by generating as much profit as possible, closing a deal, creating a strategic partnership, or successfully selling and marketing a product. In other words, truth telling as we learned it may put you at a major disadvantage in business dealings.

However, *you* draw the line. How far you push it will depend on whether or not you feel your decision will cause you to lose self-respect, personal integrity, sleep, or weigh heavily on your conscience. No one is going to want you to generate hostility or deliberately create ill-will, but you will be tested. Even though businesses will tend to respect your religion, if you allow religion to limit your thinking in the workplace, chances are the workplace will limit your opportunities for growth.

You can still be a good person within an organization, but there will be times when your moral values may be called into question. Ethics is the study of right and wrong, or more broadly, the exploration of what is good. When you're obliged to carry out an order from your boss that challenges your personal ethics you may become conflicted. But keep in mind that business is not personal, and that in this environment, decisions are made based on strategy, legality, and profit. If you become torn between spiritual versus business ethics, you may wind up stressed, with an ulcer, migraine headaches, hives, or all of the above.

The higher up the ladder you go, the more you will face ethical dilemmas, not only at your company, but at some point the dilemma may even be initiated by you. Examples of this might include:

- Your boss demands that you reprimand, terminate, or take some other action against someone on your team with which you do not agree.
- You are requested to hire or promote someone who is believed to be more energetic because of their age even though the older person has more experience and is better qualified.
- You discover that your company makes a product from substandard material so that it needs to be replaced more often, subsequently driving unnecessary consumer spending, yet yielding bigger profits.

In the workplace, you can use what you've been taught in church, at home, or at school for much of your life, but don't be limited by it as you address the ethical dilemmas you are sure to face in business.

CULTURAL CODE

Some of us may go into the business environment being self-righteous, thinking decisions will be fair, declaring there are things we will do and not do based on our religious upbringing and staunch principles, without weighing the pros and cons and allowing ourselves to bend the rules, be flexible, and play the game. Being successful doesn't have to be at odds with being spiritual. It's challenging enough that the rules of the game are constantly changing and that it takes work to keep up, but there are times when we may have to sacrifice, compromise, or modify our own personal beliefs because there are larger forces at play, namely, the corporation, and what is best for it, may not always be what's good for us. For example, we know we are deserving of a promotion or a raise and are disappointed if we don't get it. The reason for this might be solely attributed to a business strategy, namely, someone else is being groomed for that position, or there are limited re-sources, so therefore we can't take it personally. It may not seem fair, but that's the way it is. However, if you keep being passed over, that's a different story that will be addressed in another chapter. Obviously there's a problem. However, you now have two lives—life as an individual and life as a businessperson. You have to live life in both these lanes along your drive to achieve leadership success. The bottom line is we can be good people and be successful leaders at the same time.

 **MAMAisms**

- All is fair in love and business.
- There is no challenge that can overtake you when God is on your side.
- You will know the truth and the truth shall set you free.
- To thine own self be true.
- For we walk by faith, not by sight.

Not Everyone Has to Be Your BFF

We have all had to learn to "go along" to "get along" from time to time, and it's no different in the corporate workplace. While it is not usually necessary for you to betray your moral center or befriend people whom you absolutely cannot stand in order to advance, it *is essential* that you find ways to work with many different kinds of people, including people who have political, religious, or other views that may be diametrically opposite to yours. You may also have to participate on or even lead teams where people are used to very different styles of working and communicating. While it might be fun to work with the people you consider your Best Friends Forever (BFFs) and who share your likes and dislikes, you may rarely have that opportunity. You will find that it helps to identify, wherever possible, as much common ground as you can in order to bridge the gaps of individual differences. Ask yourself the following questions:

- What can I agree on with this person or group?
- What is a common goal I can establish that everyone can invest in and move toward?
- What time lines can I help to set that honor everyone's abilities and constraints?
- What resources can I help to identify that will support the team?

- How can I make assignments that ensure each member of the team can display his or her best work?
- What else can I do to make this project a success?

As you move forward in your career, we can guarantee that at least occasionally you will have to work with people who are immature, ignorant, incompetent, hostile, dangerous, or otherwise difficult (passive-aggressive, etc.). When these occasions present themselves, you must reach into your "Big Girl/Big Sister" bag of tricks and pull out interesting and inventive solutions that help you keep your sanity and still get the job done.

Sometimes a heart-to-heart talk with the challenging person can work, where you quietly sit down with the person and try to find out what is really bothering her, e.g., she doesn't really want to work on the project or believes that she had been promised some different (read, more important) role on it. Or she might be facing difficulties at home or is sick (or maybe is sick and tired of her current position), etc. Effective listening can be a great help in these instances. Be careful not to assume that you know why a person is prickly just because of the way they look, sound, or act. If you do a little research you might be surprised to learn that there is a perfectly good (or at least understandable) reason why someone is having an "off" day, week, month, or year.

At times you will have to just agree to disagree and decide to work together because the project must be done. You don't have to pretend to be the difficult person's best buddy, but you can still respect yourself and them, be professional in all of your dealings, and keep your distance except for the times you have to interface with them, and then you should "do the right thing."

CULTURAL CODE

Too often we tend to like or trust only people who look like us, or hang out with people who feel the same way we do, but in the corporate world, everyone we work or associate with really doesn't have to be identical to us. There are many different kinds of relationships and we should take advantage of all of those categories. We can benefit from getting to know and becoming comfortable with many kinds of people in many different settings and situations. We should look for opportunities to demonstrate our ability to rise above any difficult circumstances and galvanize a disparate group of individuals into a productive team.

When you can find common ground among very different people regarding a business matter, it can lead to more of an investment on their parts in getting the work done and establish you as a thoughtful and valuable leader, no matter what your actual position may be. You must create new ways to respond to complaints and criticisms (including your own) and thus ensure that you will be invited, indeed begged, to take on greater responsibilities in the workplace.

 MAMAisms

○ Sometimes you must go along to get along.
○ Keep your friends close and your enemies closer.
○ Don't put all of your business in the street.
○ You don't have to like people to get along with them.
○ Both "good" and "bad" people have lessons to teach you. Learn from them all.

Motivate Others by Playing Up
Their Strengths

As a good leader, you must not only be self-motivated but you must also be able to motivate those who work with and for you. Sometimes you can put "fire in the belly" of members of your team and move them to action by finding out what they do best and making sure that they get to do those things as a part of their assignments. For example, if a person is hypercritical and hypersensitive, perhaps you can give him the responsibility for managing the details of a particular project. And if another person is really smart but not very good at keeping up with the details, then you might ask her to work on the "mission statement" or "big idea" for the project.

First and foremost, you must have a clear vision of what you want/need your team to accomplish. You must be able to set clear expectations with helpful input from your team members. To create a winning climate, you must personally believe in what you and your team are trying to achieve, or at least respect the work you have to do so that you (and they) don't resent doing it. Communicate simply what you want to accomplish and why it is important. Be willing to give and receive honest feedback from your team and others with useful knowledge about your team's tasks and available resources. A successful team is built by leveraging individual strengths across the group and focusing them on the goals that have been set, so that the sum of the whole team's work is greater than each individual member's contribution.

If you have a people development or human resources department in your workplace, you might find some help there in assessing the strengths and skills of the members of your team. You certainly need to know enough about your fellow workers to be able to tell if they can actually do—and do well—the things they think or say they can.

You probably already know people who are very impressed with themselves and brag or boast about skill sets that they may not actually have. It could be a big mistake for you to lead a team where you don't have the right people on it and/or the people are great but their abilities don't match your team goals. Don't be afraid to trust your instincts. You can also learn from "bad bosses" (everyone has had one) what *not* to do when leading a team, such as picking favorites ("teacher's pets") and giving them responsibility for parts of the project they know nothing about or worse, don't care about. Inevitably this kind of poor leadership leads to missed goals or sloppy work.

Be quick to praise but not quick to judge when you are motivating others. Find ways to say something positive about each member of your team even if you have to work really hard to do so. There's usually at least one thing that you can say that is good about a person and her work, so find that one thing and fire up your team!

Many organizations are built for stability rather than for effective change, although change is the only constant in our society today, and there are always more changes on the horizon. When building our teams, we should make sure that the members are flexible and adaptable and ready to take on new challenges and opportunities as they present themselves. When we have great teams in place, we will always be able to operate smoothly because of our teams' "bench strength."

CULTURAL CODE

We often spend too much time criticizing others instead of looking for ways to get them moving forward. When we were growing up, many of us were in the Girl Scouts or 4-H, Jack and Jill chapters, Baptist Training Youth groups or Sunday schools or vacation Bible schools in many different denominations, and we should recall some of the lessons we learned in those organizations, including cooperation and collaboration, to help us become better leaders. Even if we were not in a formal organization, we may have organized our own in our neighborhoods, e.g., Double Dutch teams, singing groups, or stick- or streetball teams. We should cheer loudly every positive step or suggestion that is made by any member of our team and ignore, to the extent that we can, lackluster efforts or bad-mouthing the work (or lack of it) of others.

Too often we fail to encourage our team members to develop their professional skills in nontraditional ways, perhaps by taking courses on change management or seeking career coaches. Remember that ongoing candid feedback is essential to the maintenance of a good team. If a member of our team is not meeting expectations, we must let them know quickly and quietly and offer him or her an opportunity to improve. However, if improvements are not shown within the expected time frames, we must be ready to take the appropriate actions, including separating an unproductive member from our team. This is what successful leaders do.

MAMAisms

- ○ **Each one, teach one.**
- ○ **Don't leave anyone out.**

○ Everybody always has something to offer.

○ Sometimes you have to dig a little deeper to find the gold in a person. Keep your shovel handy.

○ Great leaders inspire great followers, who become even greater leaders.

Do Not Let Distractions (or a Difficult Boss) Throw You Off Course

You have probably already faced challenging situations in your lives and you will occasionally be tested in your workplace. With the right attitude, you can learn from all of "life's little tests," and the best thing to do is to embrace these challenges as opportunities to learn something new. You may have to change your mind about how you see the challenge or hardship and look at it from different points of view; that may be the hardest thing you have to do. After all, work will always have its ups and downs, but it's how you respond to these yo-yo situations and disappointments that will make the difference.

As a leader you understand that you must manage up (your boss), down (your staff), and sideways (your peers). To do this successfully, you must first learn to manage yourself. Learn to ask yourself what you want to accomplish from any situation and how those around you can help you to accomplish your goals. When you must work with a difficult person don't let their negative behaviors distract you. Look for openings to learn as much about them as you can. Your first inclination may be to stay away from them. But observe rather than avoid them. Watch their work style: what they do, who they work well with, and what they gain or do not gain in the process. Learn to work with or around them by cultivating relationships that help people observe your work and your leadership style. Find opportunities where you can demonstrate who you are and what you can do. Working on special projects, helping outside of your department, and writing reports are all ways to show your value. By learning who you are and what you have to offer, difficult people will be less likely to affect how you are perceived. This is also helpful in gaining recognition from a mentor or sponsor.

You may have a difficult or demanding manager or an extremely competitive peer who goes out of his way to make each day a test or trial. Don't worry about them. Worry about *you*! How are you approaching your work and your journey? Are you putting your best foot forward at all times? Are you keeping a record of your accomplishments in your PLN and updating it regularly? Are you asking for feedback so that you can find out how your work is valued and what things you might need to improve? If you are routinely doing these things, then you are on the right track, no matter how irritating the people you work with or for may be. At a moment's notice, you should be able to say clearly how the work you are doing is contributing to your department's goals and the mission of your organization.

To improve a relationship with a manager (and keep in mind it's your job to do so, not the other way around), ask her how she'd like to work with you, and what her expectations are—whether weekly meetings work as times for updates or if she'd prefer more frequent or impromptu meetings. Let her know you're interested in having the best possible work relationship and will do what it takes to make that happen. Just keep in mind you must always perform in a way that gains her trust and makes her life easier. You will have to gauge your manager's leadership style. Does your manager have a style where she wants you to get to the point, but you're the type of person who drones on and on and meanders in your scheduled sessions? If this is the case, you have to be perceptive and accommodate and adjust to your manager's style. You're the one who will have to do the adjusting, not your manager. If you're the type of person who gets to the point and doesn't elaborate or expand on your updates and your manager's leadership style is charismatic, preferring to start the meeting with small talk or short stories, then you should learn to do the same. Be aware. Sometimes you have to "tune-in" to a boss who is difficult and find out what makes her tick and dig deep to uncover the things that would make your relationship easier. If all else fails, and you have the kind of boss who seems less than supportive, then perhaps it's time to have what some would call a "come to Jesus meeting," to get feedback so you can turn things around and get back on track.

On those occasions when a boss is uncomfortable giving feedback or doesn't give you honest feedback, perhaps to avoid confrontation, beware. If you have a boss like this, it may be time to get advice from your sponsor or someone else in the organization whose opinion you respect or as a last resort, consider it time to move on. Bosses that fall into this category can actually prevent or block you from advancing within the organization. In this case, you have to decide what's best for you. If leadership is truly your goal and your boss is not your champion, then unfortunately you may have to move to another department, or look for another job and another boss who is supportive of your efforts and contributions.

Don't be caught off guard by distractions. Being busy at work has taken on a whole new meaning these days. With technology, you are expected to do more and do it faster and more efficiently. Although this may be true, do not let technology interruptions take you off your game. Learn how to manage your email, social networks, and other distractions in a way that works best for you. This may mean checking messages or returning calls at only certain times of the day, or finding an alternative to attending every meeting. Take a fresh look at what is taking up all your time and analyze if there is something that you can do differently. Sometimes changing how you do things will allow you to work smarter and more efficiently. And while we are mentioning technology, remember to keep your personal email messages, profiles, and other personal business off the company computers.

In order for you to become a great leader, you *must* learn how to use your time wisely and manage the expectations of others so that you are not pulled in too many directions at once. You may need to inform your friends, spouses, significant others, former colleagues, church members, and sorority sisters that you cannot take their phone calls or accommodate their "drop by" visits all through the day and evening, but they can leave you a message and you will return their calls when it is appropriate for you to do so. You also must make sure, while you are in the office, that you are not spending too much time on Facebook, Twitter, any other social networking site, or personal or community service projects, no matter how passionate you may be about them.

CULTURAL CODE

Sometimes we allow ourselves to get pulled in many different directions, being the ultimate multitasker, and we get overwhelmed. However, we can face our distractions dead-on and tackle them one by one. First, we should be honest and check to make sure we are not creating unnecessary hardships for ourselves by being irresponsible (coming in late, taking personal calls or emails too frequently during the workday, turning in incomplete or sloppy work, socializing only with people that we like, etc.). If there are any steps that we can take to improve our work product and performance, then we should take those steps before we decide that other people are stopping us from advancing.

After we have made sure that we are doing our very best work and reaching out to others to work cooperatively and collaboratively, if we find that there are still problems, then we may need to seek help from a manager, mentor, or friend. We should not be afraid to ask for assistance and should accept it gracefully when it is offered. It is hard to keep up with all the things that go on in the workplace, but as VIPs, we must never get so distracted that we fail to build and manage relationships both inside and outside the company. We must remember not to get so busy that we fail to keep our eyes and ears open for obstacles as well as opportunities. When we only operate out of habit, we often limit our ability to move forward. We must take a fresh look at how we are handling our responsibilities and be willing to make appropriate adjustments.

 **MAMAisms**

- ○ **Keep your eyes on the prize.**
- ○ **Hard times come to everybody sometime.**
- ○ **Just because she is your boss doesn't mean she is always right.**
- ○ **One of the keys to failure is trying to please everyone.**
- ○ **You can tell how big a person is by what it takes to discourage her.**

Always Try to Maintain Balance

Many of us who are succeeding in Corporate America today are doing so because of the strong work ethic our African American families have instilled in us, stemming from values, fierce pride, and a desire to prove ourselves to be as good as or better than anyone else. Because we hold these beliefs to be true as well, the pressure we sometimes put on ourselves never lets up. However, being a workaholic can backfire. Unfortunately, these factors have driven some of us to work very long hours without carving out much needed time for ourselves and our families and we are often suffering silently. Sometimes you will be respected more by not making yourself available at all hours to any- and everyone and protecting yourself and your time. While you don't necessarily want to be known as a complainer, a nonconformer, or not a team player, you *do* want to be known as a consummate professional who finds ways to get the job done while also preserving some time for a healthy lifestyle and just plain old fun.

In fact, by working all the time and not having work/life balance, you could be sending the wrong message. For example, when the head of a company was faced with making a financial decision of how to downsize, evaluating which departments were more valuable than others, he looked at the productivity across the board. At the end of the day, he made the agonizing decision to outsource the department that was working the longest hours. Why? His perception was that they couldn't get their job done within a regular work-day and decided that they needed to go. So just because you're putting in longer hours doesn't necessarily mean you're working smart or being more productive, and that your overtime is being perceived that way. Quite the contrary, the message you could be sending is that you're incompetent.

Even leaders need to make time to recharge their battery. So take a step back to look at the big picture, evaluate what you're doing right at the workplace and what areas you need to work on that need improvement. All leaders need time to reflect. This is usually how they begin to cultivate and develop a vision and map out a strategy, whether it's for something as simple as developing a new relationship, scheduling a business lunch, or how to execute the next project.

Whether or not you have a significant other and have chosen to create a family, you need to reach out to others and cultivate a support network of people who have your best interests at heart to create balance in your life. You can't be all work and no play. Find ways to exercise, stretch your mind, and cultivate your spirit. Never forget you are a VIP. Treat yourself accordingly.

Often corporate cultures have elaborate policies supporting alternative work hours and venues and family lifestyles, but be careful that they don't punish employees on a career track who actually make use of these policies. Research as carefully as you can any differences between policies and practices in your workplaces before you join them, so that you will not be surprised when your vacation plans have to be canceled because you have been "called back" to respond to the demands of a manager or client. Where possible, take full advantage of professional development, and health and exercise programs that are offered by your company. Volunteer to provide assistance to others, whether through mentoring or other kinds of programs. You'll feel better when you share some of your skills with others. Remember to put yourself on your list of people to take care of and provide for. You may be the only one who will.

CULTURAL CODE

If we're passionate about what we do, many of us tend to work long hours and when recognition doesn't happen quickly enough we feel undervalued, underappreciated, and frustrated. The first thing we need to remember is to work smarter. The second thing to remember is we need to make time for ourselves. When we do, we'll be happier at work, because we will have accomplished something for us. We need to have a life outside of work for our own satisfaction in order to be all around healthy. For example, obtain a leadership position at church, join a committee, make these responsibilities practice for your leadership role at the office. Join a board of a non-profit organization where you can bring your work skills to the table and even learn from others. Go to the gym. Not enough of us do this. Those endorphins that get produced when you work up a sweat will not only shave off calories, but give you a great sense of accomplishment as well. Learn to play golf or tennis. These are great sports that will help you build relationships with colleagues at work both male and female.

MAMAisms

○ Work smart, not hard.
○ Put some sun in your sun bank every now and then.
○ All work and no play makes you dull and may give you a heart attack.
○ Recharge your battery.
○ Girl, chill.

The N-Word: Networking

You need to know the importance of the n-word—networking, that is. Networking can be a powerful tool to help you navigate your leadership pathway. You network when you meet new people directly or through other people that you already know. But it is not just about meeting folks and collecting business cards; networking is about connecting and establishing relationships that can be beneficial to you both personally and professionally. Networking allows you to be seen outside of a work setting and affords opportunities to meet and mingle with individuals whom you might not have a chance to speak with otherwise.

While it is true you need to participate in order to be part of the corporate culture, you are not obligated to go to every event or social function just to be "seen" and "heard." Rather, you should be strategic about the functions you attend. You should ask yourself what the purpose is of the program or event, who will be there, and how attending might be of benefit to you. Perhaps it is a professional development function that will assist you in advancement. Maybe it is a strictly social function or an event your company is sponsoring, or maybe it is just some time out with colleagues. In any case, when you attend, bring business cards, your positive attitude, and be prepared to demonstrate good social skills. Look for opportunities at these events to let people know who you are and what you are about and to gather information that you may not hear about otherwise. Many informal chats at networking events widen your connections and may lead to future opportunities. Spend time listening to what others are saying and follow up with people of interest. Make a note on the back of the card of someone you may want to connect with further and then send them a note reminding them of where you met and a little about your conversation.

Networking is not just for those just starting out in the workforce. It's for everyone, no matter what level you're at or where you are along your leadership journey. In fact, it becomes increasingly more important to meet new people and maintain contacts the higher up you go. It's not an activity that decreases with time; it's an opportunity to create higher visibility and more recognition.

Consider the possibility of networking at least quarterly at an event you might not normally attend, so that you can widen your circle of contacts. If you are exploring opportunities for leadership advancement, you may find that the way up is not a straight line. It may be that you make a lateral move for a higher position and zigzag up the ladder of success.

CULTURAL CODE

Too often we tend to stick together at corporate social events, trade association meetings, conferences, and the like and move about in small groups or "cliques." Not only does this tendency work against us, it may also serve to underscore beliefs that Black people are not team players and can't function independently. We know this isn't true, just as we completely understand how much of a relief it can be when you spot another "sister" or "brother" at a corporate function. These sightings are great and we should certainly act on them by collecting their contact information and expanding our networks, but we should make every effort to move out of our comfort zones and approach people of all backgrounds, including people within our companies as well as people who don't necessarily work within our job parameters. Our networks should include people of all kinds across many industries, as we never know when we may learn of an opportunity to transition up or out and we should always be ready to make that move.

 **MAMAisms**

- Don't be afraid to turn the spotlight on yourself.
- It's not what you know, but who you know, that matters.
- It takes one to know one.
- When you need a friend, it's too late to make one.
- Networking is a contact sport: You gotta touch somebody.

Change Is Inevitable, So Be Prepared

We have all heard the old adage that "change is the only constant," and in most situations, you can certainly see the truth in that statement. But how we respond to change, both personally and professionally, will in many cases determine the outcome.

To some, change feels like crisis and is perceived as a negative. However, others see change as an opportunity to stretch and grow. The difference between the two thought processes is preparation.

Understand that some change will always happen and it should be expected. So why not be ready for the inevitable? Make a "what if" plan; a plan A and a plan B.

Begin to prepare mentally, financially, and spiritually. At work you want to plan for that next big job, but you may also want to prepare an exit strategy. We know that this may be counterintuitive when things are going well, but that is precisely the time to think about it strategically. Ask yourself what you would do next if you had to leave your current job and what you would need to do it. Make a list of your answers to these questions in your PLN and begin to put plans in place.

If it is additional information or skills you need, then begin learning them. If it is people you need to meet, begin the networking process. If you have financial concerns, start saving. Become diligent with the process and take advantage of every opportunity. You will soon discover that with the right mind-set, there are more opportunities than you think. Also remember to talk with others who have been successful going through a similar process. Learn what went well and what mistakes can be avoided.

You can also prepare for changes at work by paying attention to situations that may be affecting your field or industry. Know who your company's competitors are and pay attention to what they are doing. Research and review trends, stay active in industry associations, and network within and outside of your company.

As you get busy at work, following your plan can become less of a priority. However, with practice, you can put action steps in place that become habit. Some examples include reviewing your household budget to see where you might be able to save a few extra dollars. Also take advantage of any company benefits, services, or discounts that can save you money. Make time on your calendar at least once a month to reach out to someone you want to meet or stay connected with. Remember this does not have to be an actual meeting or a meal. Instead, it can be your sending a short note or card or information that you want to share, just to show that you are thinking of them.

Our world is constantly changing. Although you have been successful at work, the challenges you face can sometimes take you off course. You need to have new approaches, tools, and thought processes to help you navigate and develop leadership skills. Change, whether you like it or not, offers you the opportunity to step out of your comfort zone. It allows you to let go of the old to make room for the new.

People change, jobs change, styles change, and situations change, and all of these changes prevent you from "getting stuck in a rut." Being open to change may lead to more or better opportunities and help you move closer to fulfilling your goal. When you change your mind-set, you change your behavior. When you change your behavior, your life changes. Learn to not only accept change but embrace it while you facilitate your leadership journey.

CULTURAL CODE

We can make our dreams manifest by being willing to change the way we think about ourselves and our capabilities, preparing ourselves for unexpected changes at our workplace and taking steps, and the occasional leap, forward.

Oftentimes we prevent our dreams from coming to fruition because we fail to put a plan in place. Although we know in our hearts that change is inevitable, we put preparation for change on the back burner. If things are going well we don't want to "spoil it" or "jinx it" by thinking about it not working out. But putting together an alternate plan will serve us well and we must begin to think of this as getting ahead of the game. When we don't have a plan, we are limiting our choices and leaving decisions about our future career path up to others.

We will feel better about the changes we experience in the workplace when we can review the options we put in place for ourselves early on. A plan in progress does not have to be cast in stone, but it can give us ideas for opportunities that may come our way.

MAMAisms

○ **Keep your bag packed and your purse at the ready.**
○ **Always put something aside for a rainy day.**
○ **Don't put all of your eggs in one basket.**
○ **When you are too comfortable you are not growing.**
○ **God won't close a door without opening another.**

Bring Your Brand to the Table: Blend into the Crowd While Still Being Yourself

You may already have developed your personal "brand"— that style of work and the way you carry yourself that is uniquely yours. If you have not done so already, now is definitely the time to establish your signature brand. Personal branding means taking the best aspects of yourself and your skill sets and making sure that those features are always associated with you. Your brand should create a level of awareness, perceptions, images, and thoughts that people identify with you that is positive and powerful. For example, it would be great if your brand identifies you as the "out-of-the-box thinker" in your group, or the one who is "always early and helpful," no matter what the purpose of the meeting. Become an expert in an area that is important to your organization and make sure you are known as someone who is indispensable in that area. You certainly don't want to be branded as the person who is always late and giving excuses about why her tasks have not been completed. You also want to be careful not to imitate someone else's branding characteristics, unless they are actually also yours. Fake or imitation personal branding is not pretty, and you will certainly be found out as a liar or branding-identity thief if you simply copy someone else's work style without making it authentically yours.

Determine what your current reputation is and what you would like it to be. There is no need to let your current job title dictate your brand or your vision for yourself. Instead, think about how you would like to be remembered and what you want to be known for. Then begin to "live your brand" and watch how you begin to stand out from the crowd and distinguish yourself from your peers. You should never be afraid to capitalize on your differences in a positive and strategic way. Remember, if you don't create your own brand, you will almost certainly be branded by others, and you may not like the brand that is associated with you.

A really great company encourages creative thinking and embraces diversity among its workforce, so hopefully you are in a work setting where you can be yourself and be appreciated and valued by your fellow employees. The longer you work, the more you will recognize what your special strengths are and how you can add value to your organization. To truly be yourself, work cannot be your only focus. You need to take time to enjoy personal pursuits that nurture you physically, mentally, and spiritually. Your own well-being will be a source of strength and you must keep it intact in order to lead others effectively.

You should be able to nourish your hobbies—African dancing, for example, traveling internationally, tutoring children or adults in your community who have difficulty reading, or collecting works created by artists of African descent—without fear that these interests outside of work will impair your reputation at work. Rather, these special interests should help to balance you and make you more interesting to your employees.

Organizing and participating in sporting events where you are not the leader of the group or where you have to be coached by or shown "how to" by others is a good way to display your humanity and vulnerability to your team. Showing that you do not do everything well is humbling and allows people to see you (and hopefully appreciate you) in a different light.

When you expose both your skilled, strong self with your less skilled, curious, adventurous self to your employees, you may be surprised to learn that people like you more, are more willing to share themselves with you, and as a result work harder for you. People are often intimidated by what they perceive to be "perfect managers," and identify more with people who are human and flawed, just like they are.

In order to keep your personal "brand" up-to-date and real, you must regularly conduct self-audits and evaluate what in your leadership style (and life) is working well for you. By reviewing your personal traits and work habits and challenging their ongoing effectiveness, you can become a better leader of yourself and of others. Don't be afraid to experiment with changes in your approach to management, particularly where you have diverse members on your team who may need varying amounts and kinds of direction and attention.

CULTURAL CODE

Too often we believe that we must look, walk, think, act, and even smell like everyone else in order to be counted as a valuable team player with leadership potential. Instead, we often end up losing our individuality and our cultural strengths and our brand becomes a boring remake of someone else's work life and style. We must not be afraid to be ourselves, although we must also be willing to be brave enough to challenge the authenticity of our own brand. As we continue to grow and develop we can become the kind of leaders we respect most: those who are not afraid to become even better than they already are.

MAMAisms

○ Become known as the expert without overshadowing others.

○ Raise your profile to help advance your career and increase your market value.

○ Never be afraid to march to the beat of your own personal drummer, even if no one else can hear the music.

○ Brand yourself and be your brand!

○ Be yourself! That's enough.

30

You Don't Need to Have All the Answers to Take Advantage of the Opportunities

There will be times when you just don't know the answer. Know that you are not alone. This happens to everyone. Recognizing and accepting that you don't know the answer to every issue is in fact a strength and takes a level of maturity. Give yourself permission to admit you don't know.

When this happens, stop and evaluate the situation at hand. Give yourself time and space to think about the issues and consider the options, allowing you to make informed decisions. Ask yourself what information you will need in order to make an educated decision. What research is needed and how can you obtain it? Who do you know who may be able to help you?

Recognize that you are smart and trust your gut. But don't be afraid to ask for help to get the answers that you need.

CULTURAL CODE

We usually think we ought to know everything so we won't be perceived as being weak or stupid. The truth is, we usually know more than we give ourselves credit for. Thus it is important to understand and eliminate self-imposed limitations. However, to do this requires some stretch. Just know that it is so satisfying to see what we can accomplish when we step outside our comfort zones.

This is a good time to be flexible and open to learning new things and new ways of handling situations. Let common sense be our guide.

As women, we tend to pass up opportunities we feel may be over our heads. Instead, we need to practice having a can-do attitude and then be prepared to get the training and information needed to move forward using our skills, experience, and common sense. Often the rewards far outweigh the risks.

Taking advantage of opportunities such as these may mean accepting some risks. We only grow when we push ourselves beyond what we already know.

 **MAMAisms**

- ○ Smart people are not afraid to ask for help.
- ○ If you need a helping hand, you will find one at the end of each of your arms.
- ○ It's easier to ask for forgiveness than to ask for permission.
- ○ Walk by faith, not by sight.
- ○ You'll know what to do when the time comes.

What You See Is What You Create

Where there is no vision, the people perish.
—(PROVERBS 29:18)

As a woman you're naturally good at executing because you have to "do" things to get your job done. You have day-to-day tasks to perform, projects to complete, strategies to execute. You have a strong command of the details of your job and you accomplish your objectives. And when you're good at a task, chances are your company will want you to continue doing great work and keep you in that job. So be careful. As you step into bigger leadership roles the rules of the game change and you must learn to use a different set of skills. One of the things that distinguishes a good manager from a good leader is vision—a quality you must have for advancement. You must be able to stand on top of the mountain, so to speak, and have a bird's-eye view of your team, department, organization, or industry and do the following:

- Think about and anticipate events that may impact your team, organization, or industry. (Trust your intuition about developments in your field.)
- Simplify or streamline complex situations or processes, such as work flow.
- Consider new business that may help generate revenue or open new revenue streams.
- Develop new strategies.

- Identify new or unexploited opportunities in the business environment.
- Look at the competition.
- Have exchanges with people inside and outside your organization.
- Be open to new ways of doing things.
- Challenge yourself and inspire others to think out of the box, outside the status quo.
- Look at your company's mission statement and make sure your vision supports the overall mission.
- Do your research. Read books by futurists to look at emerging trends in your field. Visit websites for information and inspiration.

Ask yourself :

- What's new in my industry?
- What's different?
- What's the next big thing?
- What can we do better?
- What can we do more efficiently?
- How else can we do more?
- What's working and what's not working?

As you begin to think about your ideas to formulate your vision, write them down in your PLN. Then when you're ready, sell your vision of the future, your vision for change, with your team, and listen to their thinking in case they want to make any contributions and/or give you feedback. Then ultimately share your vision with your boss and/or stakeholders.

Being forward-looking, imagining exciting possibilities, and engaging others to share your view of the future are some of the things that distinguish leaders from nonleaders.* In fact, a recent *Harvard Business Review* study reveals that the number one requirement of a leader is "trust." But the second biggest requirement is that a leader be "forward-looking." In other words, that she be a visionary with an eye toward the future. You have to look inside yourself for vision, use your imagination, instincts, and experience to think of the possibilities. What you see becomes a vision that will lead you to create.

CULTURAL CODE

Too often we get bogged down in the day-to-day of doing a great job, running a tight ship, and playing things safe, but it's important to dream big and go out on a limb and take a risk every now and then! We tend to operate based on concrete facts, quantifiable objectives, and pride ourselves on our people skills. But creating a vision is very different than compiling data for a report, meeting sales quotas, dealing with suppliers and customers, producing commercials, or supervising inventory or client accounts. It's coming up with the big picture—a creative way of looking at the future. In fact, it's often these very talents that bring us management success in mid-level roles that can also be obstacles to us taking on bigger leadership roles. So craft a strategy based on a view of the business as opposed to a view of a function, and begin making "vision" one of the things you are known for.

By the way, all the rules that apply to creating a vision for your team, department, and organization, apply to creating a vision for yourself—for building your own brand and painting a picture of

*"To Lead, Create a Shared Vision," by James M. Kouzes and Barry Z. Posner, *Harvard Business Review,* January 2009, p.20.

who you want to be and how you want to show up as a leader—are in Chapter 29.

 **MAMAisms**

○ Name it and claim it.
○ A visionary does not follow a path; instead she goes where there is no path and leaves a trail.
○ Don't limit your success.
○ The best way to predict the future is to create it.
○ Keep your feet on the ground and your eyes on the sky.

Use Conflict as an
Opportunity to Solve Problems

Because conflict can make you feel uncomfortable you may want to avoid it. However, good leaders aren't afraid of conflict. They use it as an opportunity to take a step back to evaluate a situation and improve it. The key to resolving conflict is to look at the issues involved rather than the personalities. Once you identify these issues you must make every effort to resolve the problem by doing the homework where appropriate and within a reasonable period of time, depending upon how complex the problem is. If you don't tackle the problem within a reasonable time frame you may run the risk of costing the company money because the team may become less productive due to feelings of anxiety, stress, low morale, illness, absenteeism, resentment, or even hostility.

Interpersonal conflict always warrants a solution sooner rather than later, since this situation is also counterproductive. The healthy way to resolve interpersonal conflict is through a face-to-face conversation to discuss the issues and your feelings. Your objective is not to score a personal victory, but rather one that makes the most sense to foster collaboration with your co-worker and maintain a healthy work relationship to achieve the goals of the department. The main thing is not to hold a grudge or dwell on negativity, and above all, to keep your emotions out of the conflict-resolution process. So instead of putting a Band-Aid on conflict, dig deep and solve the problem. Coming up with a whole new solution, a new plan, or process to achieve goals will be rewarding. This is an opportunity for you to think creatively, for you to take a risk, try something new, change the status quo. Relationships are extremely important in business. And it's through your relationships that you will be guided along your leadership path, so don't burn any bridges along the way.

CULTURAL CODE

Sometimes we tend to run away from conflict and think it'll disappear, or just as bad, pretend it doesn't exist and allow it to sit there like an elephant hiding underneath a rug. Another mistake is, sometimes we think we have to resolve conflict ourselves, instead of engaging others to help. Conflict is a part of life, but it isn't always negative. There is always something to be learned from it. The rule of thumb is to listen. When we allow all sides to air their differences and we do the research, we can find some common ground to build upon, and when we have the facts we can begin to put the pieces together. Out of these differences in opinion, opportunities, and new information, new options will arise. Also, this is a good time to hone your negotiating skill and show that you can mediate difficult situations.

At the end of the day, not only does it make sense to get along with people, it's good karma to maintain and value relationships. But the reality is, in life there is conflict, and leaders need to be good at resolving it.

 **MAMAisms**

- ○ Out of chaos comes opportunity.
- ○ Every adversity brings a benefit of some kind.
- ○ You are not learning when your lips are moving.
- ○ Growth does not come without sacrifice.
- ○ No pain, no gain.

Don't Be Defeated by the Madness:
Keep Your Sanity

Never, never, never stop believing in yourself! Just don't do it. When someone criticizes you or your work, try not to take it personally and look for the nugget of useful feedback that you may actually want to use to improve your performance on your job. Everyone knows what it is like when nothing seems to be going as you planned and you begin to question how you got to a particular situation. You must learn that sometimes change happens without your realizing it or being prepared, and other times whatever is happening simply has nothing to do with you.

When there is a potentially explosive situation and a really outrageous action is taken against you—you're accused of a crime, you're laid off or terminated with prejudice, you're abruptly downsized to a completely different job that you feel is beneath you, etc.—you may be tempted to read someone the riot act, pack up your things, and walk out. We recommend that you impose a "24-hour rule" and take no immediate action, no matter how difficult this may seem. We all know of colleagues who have not waited to act and have said or done things they later regretted. If you can restrain yourself, sometimes the problem will resolve itself. Perhaps an action was taken in error, or the sender of a damaging message did not have her facts straight and was corrected by your peers or your boss. Gather as many facts as possible before you decide what to do or whether to do anything at all.

Once you have gathered all the information you can, you should speak with someone you can really trust. That person could be a peer or more senior employee who has your best interests at heart in your workplace, or may be a friend or mentor from outside your company. You must be able to be completely frank with the person you choose to confide in and you must also be able to receive the advice he or she gives you without overreacting in case you disagree.

You may ultimately decide that winning the battle is not worth losing the war. If correcting a mistaken impression about yourself or your work will make you appear to be a "nitpicker" or "whiner," you would be wise to overlook the matter. On the other hand, if a major mistake has been made that has been wrongly attributed to you or a member of your team, then you must take steps to correct that perception, even if you must take on an equal or someone more senior than you. Be sure to garner as much support as you can from your peers and higher-ups before you make your move.

Just because you decide to accept a decision with which you are not comfortable, or that appears at least initially to be unfair or just plain wrong, doesn't mean that you are a "wimp" or a "wuss" and people can now walk all over you. Business settings are rife with "land mines," some of which are not so clearly marked, and you will likely bump into some uncomfortable circumstances that you might not have been able to anticipate.

For example, a problem you might experience is being asked to supervise a new employee who is not particularly competent or considerate and who turns out to be related to your manager or someone else high up in your company. You must keep good records and give constant written feedback to your new direct report, so that you can demonstrate that you gave clear and consistent instructions to the employee that she did not or could not follow. No matter how you feel about this person, you must also give her the opportunity to improve work performance and document every instance when the goals you set are not accomplished. You may be able to consult a liaison in your human resources or people development department to see if you could arrange for the employee to be transferred to another position in the company (preferably in another department) for which she might be better suited.

There may well come a time when you will have to draw the line, whether for moral, legal, or more personal reasons. Right is right and you need not abandon your principles or beliefs in order to be a successful leader. In fact, when you decide to speak up, you may find that you are respected even more because of the courageous stand you take. Don't be afraid to trust your instincts. Whether you believe you must report an action or proposed action because of your duty under law or you just feel that the situation you are aware of isn't ethically correct, you must be prepared for the inevitable fallout that may occur and should probably speak with an attorney outside your company for advice before taking any action. If you find that someone in your company has actually broken the law, you may be required by the codes of business conduct to report the illegal conduct to the top lawyer, often called the general counsel, at your workplace. There are whistle-blower statutes in some states that protect employees who report the unlawful behavior of their fellow employees or managers, so be sure to check to see if you are protected in this manner.

CULTURAL CODE

Sometimes we may give up too soon because we are afraid. We feel beaten or defeated by our circumstances and aren't sure that we can be successful where we are. We must stay strong!

We are an amazing people who have survived many experiences

no one, not even some of us, thought we could get through. We are much more resilient than we may believe and we can certainly get past a difficult manager or work setting. In some workplaces managers make it a point to set employees against each other to try to get them to work harder to produce the best products or bring in the most revenue. This cultivation of infighting and supercompetitiveness may not bring about the best results for the company and often leads to unhappy and frightened employees. If we find ourselves in such a work setting, we must not begin to doubt ourselves and scramble to become the best "fighter" and "underminer" in the unit, particularly if that does not suit our personality and work style.

We must find out everything we can about our rights and then decide what to do. If the situation might be improved by our speaking out, then we must resolve to do so. If, on the other hand, it is clear that we are not protected and the managers of the company have no interest in doing the right thing, then it may be better for us to pick up our marbles and go home or on to the next job opportunity. We must learn to maintain our integrity and keep our dignity, whatever we decide to do.

MAMAisms

- ○ Do not let other people kill your joy.
- ○ Remember that you always have choices.
- ○ There are some battles not worth fighting, even when you win, and others that must be fought, even if you lose.
- ○ Don't let those crazies get you down.
- ○ When you do decide to fight, aim to win!

Know How to Create and Use Power

According to *Webster's Dictionary,* power is a possession of control, authority, or influence over others: the ability to act or produce an effect. Force. Energy. Strength.

Oftentimes when you think of power you immediately think of the highest-ranking person or the one in control. However, power is not only about hierarchy it is more about relationships, influence, access to and control over resources, as well as opportunity. To start, a good leader develops power by effectively building relationships, getting involved with organizational activities, with decision-making processes, generating new ideas, increasing her visibility, and expanding her role across boundaries or departments. Based on research, the following characteristics are important for holding great power in organizations:* Energy, endurance, and physical stamina; the ability to focus your energy and to avoid wasted effort; sensitivity, which makes it possible to read and understand others; flexibility, particularly with respect to selecting various means in order to achieve your goals; the willingness to engage, when necessary, in conflict and confrontation, or, in other words, a certain degree of personal toughness; the ability to submerge your ego, at least temporarily, in order to get something accomplished, and play the good subordinate or team player to enlist

*Managing with Power: Power and Influence in Organizations, Jeffrey Pfeffer, Harvard Business School Press, Boston, Massachusets, 1992.

the help and the support of others. All these traits seem to be evident in people who possess substantial power.

To acquire or create power, you must first build relationships, then use these relationships to get results to accomplish your department or company's goals. For example, if you have an idea for a new project that involves getting resources from another division and you already have a relationship with someone in that division who can collaborate with you or help you meet your objective, that's using your power. To get your manager to buy into this project, use your power to influence. Power acquisition and power use can have a direct impact on your career progress, job performance, and leadership development.

Three attributes are associated with personal power: (1) knowledge and information, which is basically your expertise, (2) personal attraction, which means your ability to get along with others, to be pleasant, and to dress professionally, and (3) your ability to get things accomplished on high-profile assignments that will enhance visibility to your manager and other senior executives. Creating power requires getting noticed. Position power will help you to achieve this. And it doesn't really matter at what level position you are as long as you are familiar with work flow and are willing to expand your communication network within and outside your department. Remember, step outside your comfort zone. Enrich your job by moving beyond routine activities, generating novel ideas, taking on high-profile projects, getting involved in the decision-making process, and increasing your interaction with senior executives. There's the story of a college intern from Atlanta who, while working for the summer, scheduled fifteen-minute meetings with three senior executives at a corporation, including the CEO. Within months after graduating from college, she landed an entry position in the marketing department at another division within the same corporation. And yes, it was networking, but without realizing it, this young sister was using her power, turning it into influence to secure a job—and it worked.

To increase your level of visibility, there are a few things you can do. Get on a task force that has relevance to goal-setting initiatives at your company. All companies have them, but may not think that you're interested in participating, so let others know that you are. Don't just join, but actively participate in professional and community groups, and use your networking skills to build critical relational contacts. Visibility is the key to forming strategic alliances. The more alliances you have, the more power you create, and the more you will be able to influence the behavior of others because the goal of any leader is to get followers to collaborate on achieving an objective ultimately tied into accomplishing your organization's goals.

A powerful person can get things done and make things happen. She has the ability to motivate herself and others and effect decisions and results. Learning to identify the power that you have and utilizing it in an effective manner takes a strong sense of self and a level of maturity. However, even with these traits, the "power game" may not come naturally to you. As a woman you may think that "power" is something that men have, that it's not for you.* However, a Simmons School of Management survey reveals that 80 percent of women indicated that they were comfortable with power, respected it, and liked what they could accomplish with it. Interestingly enough, these findings also suggest that women are less comfortable with traditional models of power over others, but are comfortable in exercising power with and through others.

Overall, there are several basic skill strategies that must be contin-

*"Women Pursuing Leadership and Power: Challenging the Myth of the Opt Out Revolution," Deborah Merrill-Sands, Jill Kickul, Cynthia Ingols, Center for Gender in Organizations (CGO). Linking gender and organizational effectiveness, CGO Insights, Simmons School of Management, Boston, MA, 2005.

ually practiced to be an effective power player in the workplace. Once these skill strategies are mastered, you will be able to apply them as needed. Patience, determination, credibility, emotional intelligence, relationship building, and a sense of curiosity are all important when creating and using power. People want to follow a good leader and want to be around one that is powerful.

In addition, many studies reveal that women in power face a double-edged sword as the attributes that often serve male leaders well in this regard (assertiveness and self-promotion) tend to undermine a woman's influence. This problem continues to be a difficult balancing act especially for women of color; however, combining various leadership styles helps in this regard.

CULTURAL CODE

Sometimes we tend to give away our own personal power because we may feel powerless. Perhaps this is because we don't know how to create and utilize power or understand why it is important to have. Power and influence should continually be developed and practiced regardless of your position within an organization. If you have not already done so, begin developing the basic skills needed to be a power player. Make sure you do so in a manner that does not exhibit arrogance. But understand that getting work done with and through others, even without authority, is a good way to practice your power and effective leadership skills. All good leaders must influence and we must learn not to give our power away by letting others affect our mood or frustrate and anger us.

MAMAᴉꜱᴍꜱ

○ Use what you got to get what you want.
○ Real power comes from relationships.
○ Don't let your power go to your head.
○ Preach with your life rather than your lips.
○ Own the power that you have.

35

No One Leadership Style Fits All: Know When to Mix It Up

Good leaders need a variety of leadership styles to be successful. There is no one way to manage a team. However, to learn the style that will work best in any given situation takes knowing yourself as well as the individuals you are working with. Different situations will require different styles of management. A demanding authoritative style may be necessary on one occasion and a democratic, consensus-building style on another, while transactional-style may work best at another time. One style may feel more like a natural fit for you, but as a leader, you should know how to utilize all of these styles because the wrong style for the wrong situation can lead to harmful results, including unhappy employees.

Pay attention to your style of leadership and note which style works best and for which situation. Be resilient and look for options so that if one style does not work in a situation, you can try another. Notice how your employees react to your approach and which ways yield the best results. Don't be afraid to mix it up.

Over the years many styles of leadership have been identified and described. Here are the most popular and widely used. See which one or two styles describe how you operate the best:

- Authoritarian. Also known as autocratic leadership. This style is used when leaders tell their employees what they want done and how they want it accomplished without getting advice or suggestions from them. This style of leadership should not be used often since it can lead to resentment and high staff turnover. But there may be times when there's an urgent request or demand to accomplish a specific goal or a task in a particular way that can make this style appropriate.

- Charismatic. A leadership style where an individual uses enthusiasm and high energy to drive others to achieving goals.
- Transactional. These leaders make sure the routine work gets done. It's really just a way of being a supermanager, because it focuses on the completion of short-term tasks. Oftentimes it's combined with transformational leadership.
- Transformational. In this leadership style, the person inspires her team with a vision of the future. This leader helps team members look at the big picture for the good of the team. They make workers feel that what they are doing contributes to a broader purpose, helping them look beyond self-interest.
- Participative. Also known as Democratic, where the leader encourages the team to speak up and express their opinions to contribute to the decision-making process. This not only increases job satisfaction by involving employees in what's going on, it gives them a sense of ownership in the process. Even though you're the one making the final decision, casting that final vote, everyone gets to have a say, which makes them more engaged in the process and more motivated. In general, this is the most effective leadership style.
- Bureaucratic. These leaders work by the book, making sure staff follows procedures exactly. This style leaves very little room for creativity and innovation. It is used in areas where large sums of money are handled (i.e., banks or accounting firms), or in industries where there are serious safety risks, such as working with machinery or toxic waste.
- Delegative. In this style, the leader allows the team to make the

decisions. This is used when employees are able to analyze the situation and determine what needs to be done and how to do it. This style is used when you fully trust and have confidence in your team. Ultimately, you are still responsible for the decisions that are made.

- Situational. When a decision is needed, an effective leader will use her best judgment depending upon the particular situation or a range of situational factors. Some of these factors may include the motivation of followers, followers knowing what to do and how to do it, availability of tools, resources, support, goals involved, etc.

There is no one "right" way to lead that suits all situations that you will encounter. You are not expected to use one style of leadership. Chances are you will use many if not all of these styles at one point or another. By understanding these leadership styles, their impact on others, and when to use them, you can become a more flexible, better leader.

CULTURAL CODE

Sometimes we don't look at our options. We use one leadership style, perhaps two, and get stuck or complacent without exploring other ways to motivate others to succeed and inspire them to do what is needed to get the job done. Think about the type of leader you want to be and the type of leaders you have worked with. Make a conscious effort to be the best leader you can be by looking at the various situations you encounter and knowing the best way to respond.

 **MAMA**ISMS

○ When one way doesn't work, try something else.
○ Don't get stuck in the mud.
○ Do whatever it takes to get the job done.
○ Believe in yourself; trust your instincts.
○ If at first you don't succeed try, try again.

36

Coaches Are Not Just for Athletes

If you have gotten this far in your career without the benefit of an executive coach, you have missed out on a great opportunity. Years ago, coaches were used to fix bad behavior at the top. Today, they are used by individuals who want to improve their job performance and by companies who want to develop their high potentials.

The best professionals in any given craft accept input, feedback, and guidance from their coach for continuous improvement . . . why not you? In sports, coaching helps athletes become the best. In business, they give individual attention to what you do and guide you through the process needed to reach your full potential.

A coach often provides knowledge, opinions, judgment, and constructive feedback that you may have never heard before and listens, lends support, guides, collaborates, and helps you strategize on moving forward. With a background in human resources, psychology, and/or consulting, a coach should definitely be one of the people on your success team.

Personal growth comes from asking honest questions, putting a plan in place, and then following through on that plan. Based on this, a coach can help remove blind spots, help you formulate your next steps, build on your strengths, and identify and develop areas that may not be as strong.

Unlike a mentor, a coach helps you decide what career aspects are important to you and helps you to focus on them. The coach's job is to help diagnose areas of your skills and behavior that you want or need to further develop for continued professional growth and advancement. The coach will strategize with you to enhance your personal development. Contrary to some beliefs, working with a career coach does not mean your behavior needs to be "fixed," but rather that you or your company want to invest in your leadership potential.

Oftentimes you are so busy building your career that you may miss opportunities that are available to you. Working with a coach can offer insight and different perspectives which you may not have previously thought about or discussed. To get the most out of coaching, you need to have the desire and the commitment to learn and grow. To maximize your coaching experience, you also need to have good chemistry with the individual. Before working with a coach you may want to get references, confirm her certification or accreditation, and talk to a few people she's coached to get a sense of her methodology, helpfulness, and success rate.

Do not rule out offering your team the benefit of working with a coach. Offering this individualized attention from an expert shows that you value their development and want to encourage them to reach their full potential as well.

CULTURAL CODE

We have hidden assets within that once tapped can yield tremendous results when unleashed to full capacity.

It is possible that as women, especially Black women, we have not been given critical feedback to fully explore our strengths and expose our blind spots. There are a number of reasons why this might be the case. However, some of us have not demonstrated that we are open to constructive criticism or willing to accept feedback in general. Instead of listening and evaluating the points that are being made, some of us become defensive, emotional, and accusatory and therefore miss opportunities to learn about our blind spots. We all have them and over time, the cost of remaining at the status quo could be detrimental to us in our professional life.

If you have not yet worked with a coach or an objective third party, it is wise to do so as an effective way for you to brainstorm in a confidential, objective environment. We should think of a coach as yet another tool in our leadership tool kit.

 **MAMAisms**

- ○ Leadership and learning go hand in hand.
- ○ When the student is ready the teacher appears.
- ○ Always put your best foot forward.
- ○ You're never too old to learn.
- ○ If you always do what you have always done, you will always get what you have always gotten.

Celebrate Your Arrival at the C-Suite

Congratulations! You have worked hard, navigated the culture, networked, smiled, actively listened, asked for and accepted feedback, and you are now sitting in the Corporate Suite.

Now what?

If you are lucky, there are other women who look like you who are there to greet you with open arms, but this may not always be the case. *BAM!* Wake up! Get over it! Now more than ever is when you need to count on your personal *success team*. Those people you can trust for guidance, support, collaboration, and motivation.

First, celebrate your accomplishments, then, spend some quality time reviewing and reflecting on all you have learned and how you have grown as a leader. Then it is time to get busy planning for more major accomplishments.

No, you don't have the luxury of resting on your laurels . . . you have work to do, people to see, and places to go! The most successful executives are those who continue to build and maintain support among all their key stakeholders. And because you practiced this behavior before you got the job, it will be helpful to continue it while you're on the job. Never underestimate the value and the power of relationships. The energy you spend building them will make you a better leader—and a better person.

If you have not already done so, decide what you want your legacy to be—how you want to be remembered—and start working that plan. All of the skills you possess are needed even more now. Your accomplishments to this point will now take on new meaning. Rather than just thinking about what you have done thus far, you now have to analyze the impact of what you have done—what values you bring to the table and how you will now demonstrate them.

Plan to do research and pay attention to others in the C-Suite that have been successful and note what they do well. Also pay attention to those who have failed and find out why. Determine who you need to know and who needs to know you and "go get them."

CULTURAL CODE

We know that for the most part, the higher we move up the corporate ladder, the less help we may receive internally. It is assumed that if we made it this far, we already know how the game is played. Even if the rules change, few if any are likely to tell us.

This is all the more reason to have members of our *success team* to talk to and run things by. At this point, the last thing we can afford to become is complacent. We cannot sit on our laurels and we cannot get too busy to network with individuals inside and outside our company who are also at the senior level. Although we have demonstrated time and again that we are smart, talented, professional women, we sometimes forget that we are never too old or too senior to learn something new. We neglect to develop a written plan of action for our first ninety days and then periodically thereafter whenever we are entering a new position. This is a big mistake, especially when there are often no formal feedback procedures in place. But we must not be fooled as we are surely being informally evaluated. We are reviewed to see if we are staying within budget, meeting target goals, and increasing our department's bottom line. So we must be aware of the current status in these areas and plan accordingly. We must always keep our eyes open and our ear to the ground. Plan to work and work your plan.

 **MAMAisms**

- ○ You have every right to be there—savor the experience.
- ○ It is lonely at the top.
- ○ Always watch your back.
- ○ Don't apologize for your success.
- ○ Only by going too far will you find out how far you can go.

Maintain Your Seat at the Table:
Here's What It Takes

Now that you are at the table, use your position wisely. You have earned it, so command your seat. As a C-Suite executive you will need to consistently use all the skills that you have developed thus far in this leadership role. But remember to keep your eyes and ears open. Look, listen, and learn because what got you to this point will not keep you here. Condition yourself to listen to not only the business issues being discussed but also the everyday chitchat. Take note of what motivates others and what pushes their buttons. At this level, heightened awareness is imperative. Establish friendly relationships with employees at all levels including assistants, receptionists, and mail room and cleaning staff.

In order to be successful you will need to master a wide range of behaviors. Flexibility, adaptability, and focus are the name of the game here. You must manage change, build and mend relationships, identify and utilize the expertise of others, and ensure that you have the support of your peers, all while managing yourself, your staff, your boss, and others. Maintaining a seat at the table is not only about you. Ask your peers for ideas about how you can be a great team player. Get their suggestions, but walk a fine line: You don't want to focus on being "liked" or appear to want their "approval" and risk coming off as being weak, and you don't want to appear as being "authoritarian" and risk coming off as being disrespectful. If it applies, getting customer feedback will give you insights and be helpful to your performance as well.

Having a seat at the table brings other responsibilities and priorities thrown your way and requires you to guide others that may not yet be at the level that you are. This is also a perfect time to conduct a self-audit:

- Review your strengths and build on them.
- What do you most enjoy doing?
- What has worked well for you? Identify opportunities for improvement.
- What adjustments in your work/personal style would you like to make?
- Get follow-up feedback from your manager/senior executive to ensure you're making progress.

Determine what you want to accomplish in this role and how you can effect change and bring others along while you also continue to progress. With few exceptions, your confidence, your motivation, and even your integrity will be challenged during this time. But it is imperative that you keep your sense of mental, physical, and spiritual balance. It is not unusual to feel alone and overwhelmed during this time. Just remember that your trusted friends, family, and advisers can be helpful. Sometimes just speaking about the issues will keep you on course. And don't forget to celebrate your accomplishments. Look the part of a leader, act the part of a leader, and know that your attitude and how you react to every situation is being looked at and monitored.

Of course there will be times when situations are not as you would like. Sometimes you may be asked to make tough decisions that a senior executive doesn't want to deal with—cutting budgets, reducing staff, canceling projects, hiring from the outside, not giving preference to an internal candidate for promotion, etc. During these times it pays to evaluate the benefits of your position and determine if they outweigh the challenges. Ultimately you'll need to do what's right and best for the organization, even if it means laying off a veteran employee, someone you've had a long-standing relationship with. No one said it was going to be easy at the top.

CULTURAL CODE

As a leader you will be pulled in many directions both personally and professionally. Oftentimes we are so overwhelmed and busy trying to stay on top of our game that we begin to neglect ourselves, our network, and our social circles. We have little time or energy for community involvement. Our friends, family, and those we have met and need to stay connected with rarely hear from us. This is the time when we should be most visible, but we are often buried in work. We think we can do it all and we often suffer for it. Instead, this is a time when we should capitalize on our success.

Renew memberships to organizations that you may have allowed to lapse while you were busy climbing the ladder. Join corporate or nonprofit boards, speak on panels, write articles, etc. Make sure that your name and face are out there.

Remember to keep your skills and your team's skills relevant. Continue to invest in your development and that of your team as you will be judged not only by your performance but theirs as well.

Make sure that you are the best leader you can be and strive to always bring your A game to the table.

As you lead, you should leave a personal footprint.

Remember you are leaving a legacy.

MAMAISMS

○ To whom much is given, much is required.
○ Make what you do matter.
○ Successful leadership is more about influence than control.
○ You can do anything, but you can't do everything.
○ Take the bitter with the sweet.

Seeing the Writing on the Wall

There may come a time when you no longer want a seat at your current table. This may be because you are not being treated as you think you should be because you have hit the glass ceiling, or because you are no longer challenged. Whatever the reason, there are usually signs that changes are happening and it is best for you to recognize the handwriting on the wall. Many will say that you should be planning for your next job soon after you land in your current one. However, if you have not done so, now is the time to develop a plan. Take some time to evaluate what is currently happening in your industry, in your field, in your company, and in your life that could have an impact on your next career move.

If you have been in your position for more than six months and have not developed an exit strategy, spend some time putting one in place now. If you already have a written plan, spend time reviewing it and making updates as needed.

As hard as it may be, try to take the emotion out of this process. Even if you feel that you are being treated unfairly, remember that emotion clouds your vision and usually causes you to react in an inappropriate fashion. If you are feeling frustrated or stuck, try to determine the specific reasons. Put pen to paper and start developing your plan should you want to leave or you are asked to go.

- Think about what you would like your next career move to be: possible new companies, new industry, new location, etc.
- Think about what has worked well for you in your current organization and what you would like to avoid in the future.
- Think about your strengths and what opportunities might exist that play to them.
- Think about who you know that may be of help to you during a transition and who you need to meet or reconnect with prior to leaving your current position.
- Prepare any documents that need updating: résumé, bio, profile, corporate photo, etc.
- Get the right message to the right people. Create a core message about yourself that decision makers will remember.
- Review your accomplishments and update where necessary, including dates, project names, etc.
- Organize those items that you will need to refer to during your transition, including your database of contacts.
- Contact professionals who you may need to help you with your next steps (executive search firms, executive coach, financial planner, accountant, lawyer, etc.).

Learn from others who have gone through this experience by asking questions, listening, and learning.

Start preparing a list of items that you may want the company to provide and that you can use during your negotiations. Don't be afraid to think outside the box.

Remember to treat your parting from the company like a business separation.

Remain professional and in charge of your attitude.

CULTURAL CODE

Sometimes we get too comfortable in our current work situation and neglect to see that things are changing and that we have choices. We get so busy doing what we do, we forget to take time to smell the roses and to ask ourselves if what we are doing and where we are doing it still works for us. We get stuck in our comfort zone and then become hesitant, lazy, or fearful about stepping out and trying something new. We forget or don't realize that change is an opportunity to experience new challenges. If we have our plan in place and remember to learn from adversity as well as our successes, making a move may not be as uncomfortable as we might think.

 MAMAisms

○ **Learn to read the tea leaves.**
○ **If at first you don't succeed, figure out what went wrong and try again.**
○ **Painful lessons usually turn out to be blessings in disguise.**
○ **It is what it is.**

Reach Back and Bring Others Along

No matter how smart and talented you are, you did not become a successful VIP without the help of others. Maybe you had mentors or sponsors in your workplace or a group of trusted advisers as part of your *success team*, but you had to have help to get to the level you are today. If you have not done so already, now is the time for you to reach back and help others achieve their leadership goals. You owe it to yourself and to those on whose shoulders you stand to help others. Giving back can be done in a number of ways. Mentoring, donating your time, giving advice and feedback, exposing others to new opportunities and experiences, serving on boards of nonprofit organizations, leading neighborhood groups—these are all ways you can contribute to your communities.

You are already a role model for others, whether you are aware of it or not. As a professional Black woman, you are conspicuous in your workplace and others are watching you to see how you handle yourself and your responsibilities. A great way to help younger associates is to mentor them one-on-one or in small groups. Although becoming a mentor is a big responsibility, you should do it whenever you can. As a trusted counselor for a younger employee, you can listen, guide, and "show them the ropes" so they can move ahead. Being a mentor should not be taken lightly, as it means giving of your time and expertise and opening doors whenever possible.

Too often individuals in the workplace are not given feedback on their performances and amble through their careers unaware of their strengths or weaknesses. As a mentor, you can give this valuable feedback or help the younger employees obtain it from their managers. Sometimes you may notice that an individual who is not your employee or mentee is making a mistake or is perceived in a negative way by others. Although it might be tricky, you may want to take that person aside and quietly let her know how she is thought of by her fellow workers, so she can change or expand upon those perceptions.

Invite individuals to accompany you to organizational meetings, receptions, and other venues that they may not know about so they can learn new skills and meet new people. Sharing this access to important events with others is a great way of giving back.

Although you're working very hard and time is often of the essence, you will feel so much better when you share some of your time and experience with others. Remember that giving back is the rent you pay for living on this earth!

CULTURAL CODE

Sometimes we feel that we don't need to help others because we have had so little help ourselves and have the attitude "If I can do it, someone else can do it, too." Especially if we have had a very difficult time at our workplaces (where we are the only "one" or are part of a small group of diverse employees), we may feel that "I've got mine" and "You've got yours to get." Occasionally we hear of a sister or brother who says, "No one helped me, so why should I help anybody else?" Even if we couldn't see the helpers, we must always remember that many people sacrificed a great deal so that we could have the opportunities we have now to work where we want and climb the corporate ladders of success. We know that other groups help one another to achieve and why shouldn't we do the same for our own? We know how hard it can be out there for a sister and we owe it to ourselves and one another to help others whenever possible.

That doesn't mean that we have to trust everyone who looks like us with all of our innermost secrets. It does mean, however, that we should always be willing to offer a helping hand, share our knowledge and share our contacts. Even the small things we can do, like making a phone call or stopping by someone's office just to say hello, can make a huge difference in someone else's life. We should be willing to share what has worked well for us as well as the pitfalls we have encountered and how we overcame them.

Many cultures give back to those within their groups, not feeling the threat of sharing knowledge due to insecurity or competition like crabs in a barrel. We need to make reaching back and bringing others along a tradition, too.

We realize that passing the torch of leadership success is important and we want to celebrate our accomplishments as well as those of the coming generations of Black women leaders. Always be willing to reach back to help young sisters coming along. Help them do well in their current position and prepare for their next steps. Know that helping others helps us to grow. And if you believe in karma, reaching back and bringing others along is a very good thing.

As those of us in the old guard step down and begin to retire and a new emerging group of dynamic young leaders falls into line, instead of starting the lessons all over again, it's imperative to take advantage and benefit from the knowledge, advice, and expertise of those who have come before. According to a recent Simmons School of Management study, 85 percent of women of color, compared to

70 percent of white women, aspired to be influential leaders.* Yet these numbers aren't reflected in the corporate and noncorporate environments. And that will be even more apparent if younger women don't come to seasoned Black women executives to seek advice.

It is our hope that this book will help us to guide one another so we can all reach our leadership potential for generations to come. In this way, we can increase our numbers and therefore our influence and power, taking up more real estate in the C-Suite, permanent seats at the table, and even more seats at the head of the table. Now that would be victorious. Now that would make all of our MAMAs proud!

 MAMAisms

- ○ Each one teach one.
- ○ Contribute to something larger than yourself.
- ○ No gift is too small—do what you can.
- ○ I have because I give, I give because I have, therefore I am never without.
- ○ Pass the torch.

*"Women Pursuing Leadership and Power: Challenging the Myth of the Opt Out Revolution," Deborah Merrill-Sands, Jill Kickul, Cynthia Ingols, Center for Gender in Organizations (CGO). Linking gender and organizational effectiveness, CGO Insights, Simmons School of Management, Boston, MA, 2005.

ACKNOWLEDGMENTS

The authors would like to individually thank the following who have helped them tap into their leadership potential:

Elaine Meryl Brown:
I'd like to thank my mother, Ethele; my sister, Erica; and my niece, Madison, only six and already leading me around. I'd like to thank all the ancestors in my family upon whose shoulders I stand, as well as all the mentors I've had along the way: Ina Siler, Dr. Robin Johnson, Dr. David Porter, Kathy Johnson, Toni Fay, Adriane Gaines, Yanna Kroyt-Brandt, Sheryl Tucker, Marsha, Rhonda, and others and you know who you are. Special thanks to Alex, Morgan, Joe Rojas my technology guru, and to Nate who is always there to listen. To my son, David, for whom I've always tried to set an example for working and living.

Marsha Haygood:
I'd like to thank my mom, Elverso Hook, who taught me all that I know, who told me that I was smart and could do anything I wanted and I believed her. And thank you to my big sister, Shirley, for always being there for me. Thank you to my sons Hart, Gregory, Kenny, and Shawn for keeping me on my toes. Special thanks to Franz, my technology lifesaver. And most of all, thank you, my husband Donald, for all your love, support, and guidance and for en-

couraging me to be the best that I can be. And last but not least, thank you, Elaine, for inviting Rhonda and me to join you in this life-changing project.

Rhonda Joy McLean:

This book, my first, is dedicated to my three grandmothers (yes, I had three!)—Madeline Roberta Alexander, Cora Avery Boyd, and Eva Belle Coleman Coles. Your shining examples of strength, spice, and grace continue to light my way.

I would like to thank my parents, John Wesley and Georgianna Virginia McLean, for the amazing constancy of your love that has always been there for me, and, thank God, continues to be so. Thanks also to the many members of my family, both real and extended, for your unswerving support along my journey.

I simply must thank my life partner, Bill, for embracing me and all my eccentricities and dazzling me with love.

Elaine, Marsha, and Rhonda:

We would like to collectively thank the wonderful and generous ladies of the Girls Night Out (GNO) Experience, who never fail to lift us up, make us laugh, and inspire us to just get on with life and living! To Angela Burt-Murray, thanks for your encouragement and for taking the time to write our Foreword. We'd like to thank our fabulous agent, Laura Ross, who immediately understood the importance and value of our book and its relevancy to Black women around the world, for whose amazing enthusiasm and support we will always be grateful. To Alice Peck, who never stopped believing and never stopped being our cheerleader. We would also like to thank Porscha Burke, who as a young sister at Random House/Ballantine anxiously grabbed on to our book like a kid in a candy store, whose bright eyes lit up with excitement, as if we had written this book just for her. And of course Melody Guy, our editor at Random

House/Ballantine, who upon reading the proposal saw the potential and need for a book like ours and with great care and sense of urgency, immediately rushed it through to publication to get into the hands of the many thousands of Black women with leadership potential and those transitioning their way to becoming master leaders seeking a seat at the table. We thank all of you for everything—the kindness, the care, the love.

ABOUT THE AUTHORS

ELAINE MERYL BROWN, vice president special markets and Cinemax Group, at HBO, is an Emmy Award–winning writer and executive producer, and has won numerous awards in the broadcast industry. She was creative director at Showtime Networks and has worked in television at both the national and local level. In 2007, Brown was chosen as one of *The Network Journal*'s "25 Influential Black Women in Business." Brown is the author of two novels, *Lemon City* and *Playing by the Rules,* and is currently working on a young adult fiction series. She is a Wheaton College alumni/trustee and a graduate of NAMIC's UCLA Anderson School of Management Executive Leadership Development Program, as well as the CTAM Executive Management Program at the Harvard Business School. Brown is a member of the National Association for Multi-Ethnicity in Communications, New York Women in Film and Television, PRO-MAX (an organization for marketing, promotion, and design professionals within the entertainment/information industry), and Cable & Telecommunications Association for Marketing. Born in Harlem, she now resides in New Jersey.

MARSHA HAYGOOD is a dynamic career and personal coach and a powerful motivational speaker on topics such as leadership success. After a twenty-five-plus year career in human resources, Haygood founded StepWise Associates, LLC, a career and personal development consultancy. Prior to that, she was executive vice president of Human Resources and Administration at New Line Cinema (a division of Time Warner), and has held executive positions at Orion Pictures Corp., among other companies. A graduate of Lehman College she also holds certification in Training and Development from New York University. Haygood serves on the board of directors of Youth-Bridge NY, a nonprofit high school leadership development organization, and is a senior advisory board member of the National Association of African Americans in Human Resources. She is a member of the Society of Human Resources Management and the National Association of Female Executives. Haygood has won numerous awards including the YMCA Black Achievement Award and the National Association of African Americans in Human Resources Trailblazer Award. In 2005 she was honored by *The Network Journal* as one of the "25 Influential Black Women in Business." Haygood was featured in the first edition of *Speaking of Success: World Class Experts Share Their Secrets,* alongside such authors as Stephen Covey, Ken Blanchard, and Jack Canfield. She and her husband reside in New York and Florida.

RHONDA JOY MCLEAN is deputy general counsel of Time Inc. and the former assistant regional director of the Northeast Region of the Federal Trade Commission. She received her J.D. from Yale Law School in 1983 and was elected to the Yale Law School Fund board of directors in 2008. She has served as chair of the Yale Law School Alumni Association and is currently the treasurer of the board of directors of the Better Business Bureau of Metropolitan New York. Before attending Yale, Ms. McLean received her M.S. degree from North Carolina A & T State University and a B.A. from Aurora University. In March 2007, McLean was named by *The Network Journal* as one of the "25 Influential Black Women in Business" and is a recipient of the Ruth Whitehead Whaley Public Service Award by the Association of Black Women Attorneys in recognition of her mentoring more than 100 young women attorneys. McLean was given the Black Achievers in Industry Award from the Harlem YMCA in

2002 and the Woman of Power and Influence Award from the New York Chapter of the National Organization for Women in 2003, among many other honors and tributes. McLean was born in Chicago, Illinois, and reared in Smithfield, North Carolina. A classically trained pianist and mezzo-soprano, she performs sacred music with chorales in the New York metropolitan area, where she resides.

ABOUT THE TYPE

This book was set in Delima, a typeface designed by Ong Chong Wah (b. 1955) for the Monotype Corporation in 1993. Delima's generous x-height (the difference between the baseline and the meanline in a typeface; typically, the height of the letter x) and open characters give this face exceptional legibility at small sizes and an even color on the text page.